you & your wedding

The
BRIDE'S
Book

you & your wedding®

The BRIDE'S Book

Carole Hamilton

foulsham
LONDON • NEW YORK • TORONTO • SYDNEY

foulsham

The Oriel
Capital Point
33 Bath Road
Slough
Berkshire SLI 3UF
England

For Nick and George

Foulsham books can be found in all good bookshops and direct from www.foulsham.com

ISBN: 978-0-572-03316-3

Printed in Dubai

Design: Matthew Inman

Contents

Congratulations!

You're engaged and the countdown has begun towards the momentous moment when you marry the man you love. Get ready to start planning your wonderful wedding day!

This is something you may have been dreaming about since you were a little girl, or perhaps have only recently thought about now you have met the man you want to marry. Either way, you're about to start a period of wedding obsession.

As editor of *You & Your Wedding* magazine for more than 13 years, I met every possible kind of bride-to-be. On the one hand, I came across girls with complete wedding scrapbooks, details planned to perfection before they had even met their man. On the other, I met girls who had literally a few weeks to go and hardly a decision had been made. Hopefully you are somewhere in between and, since you are reading this book, I am presuming that you want some help – which is where I come in!

Weddings have a head-in-the-clouds quality all of their own but they need to be planned and paid for in the real world, which is why I've made this book as down-to-earth as possible. I'm a great believer in individuality and have been stunned during my time on the magazine by how creative couples can be, often on a tight budget. Believe me when I say there is no right or wrong way to plan a wedding and that the most memorable weddings are not about money. What your guests will remember are the little touches that obviously mean a lot to you... your sister's tear-filled reading, your best friend singing a love song, your tiny niece scattering petals down the aisle.

My single piece of advice to anyone planning a wedding is: enjoy it. Yes, there will be highs and lows, family fallings-out and times when you wonder why on earth you ever started on the long road down the aisle. But try to keep it all in perspective. Your wedding day is going to be wonderful! **Carole Hamilton**

Kathryn Lloyd &
Stephen van Rooyen

Hotel Tresanton,
Cornwall

Hotel Tresanton

Chapter *1*

It All Starts Here

He popped the question and you said yes!
Your adventure is about to begin. Once you
come down from cloud nine and announce
your happy news, the first things you will
need to address are the date and the style of
your wedding.

Do you want a long engagement? Or do you fancy getting married as soon as possible? The average engagement in the UK is currently around 16 months according to the latest statistics, but you can organise everything a lot quicker or take a lot longer; it really is whatever suits you best.

Many couples choose to share the news of their engagement by putting an announcement in the local and/or national newspapers. Typically, the announcement is made by the bride's parents and is simply worded. For example:

Mr and Mrs John Smith of Ruislip, Middlesex
are delighted to announce the engagement of their daughter Claire
to Robert Jones of Maidstone, Kent
A June 2008 wedding is being planned

You don't have to mention a wedding date if nothing has been planned and the groom's parents may like to put a similar engagement announcement in their local newspaper as well.

Formal engagement parties are not as popular as they once were, mainly because the majority of couples are already living together before they become engaged. But if you want to hold an informal bash to celebrate your forthcoming nuptials, then go ahead; just make it clear on the invitations that gifts, while appreciated, are certainly not expected. Engagement presents were traditionally the first step for cash-strapped couples to get together basic household items but, for many modern couples who already have most of the basics, gift giving really isn't necessary.

Keeping your sense of humour

A word of caution to you as a newly engaged couple: be prepared for a few ups and downs, particularly in the early days of your engagement. You are bound to get the 'aren't you too young to get tied down?', 'are you expecting a baby?', 'do you really know him well enough to marry him?' type of questions. You'll also find friends and family offering all manner of advice and recommendations, from the best dressmaker to their favourite florist. You will probably have more than one person dropping heavy hints about how they'd just love to be your bridesmaid/best man.

Weddings are exciting for everyone and most people are just trying to be helpful. Learn to keep your cool and don't agree to anything without giving it careful consideration first. At the same time, try not to become too smug about your newly engaged status. Some of your friends may feel a little jealous and worry about losing your friendship as you move towards the big day. And be patient with co-workers who don't want to live and breathe your wedding plans every minute of the day – not everyone is as excited as you are!

> ### *Real Bride's Hot Tip*
> *One friend became very distant for a while but, once I asked her to be my bridesmaid and involved her in my plans, she went back to being my best mate.*
> **Sara Powell, London**

What type of ceremony?

The most important part of the wedding day is, of course, the marriage ceremony – that magical moment when you exchange your vows and become husband and wife. But which style of marriage ceremony is for you? This is one of your key decisions and needs to be confirmed before you think about anything else.

You have three basic choices for your marriage ceremony in England, Northern Ireland and Wales: a church wedding; a civil wedding in a licensed building; or a civil wedding in a register office. The law in Scotland is less rigid and allows for the ceremony to be performed just about anywhere. There's no right or wrong choice; it largely depends on whether you have any religious convictions.

If you decide on a civil ceremony, which of the two types you choose is down to practicality and budget. A register office ceremony is quick and informal and allows you to have a reception anywhere you like. A civil ceremony in a licensed building costs more but allows you to hold the whole wedding in one place.

Another option is to get married abroad. This is becomingly increasingly popular, with an estimated 30,000 couples from the UK now travelling abroad to tie the knot. The lure of a far-flung beach is great, with the Indian Ocean and the Caribbean topping the list of favourite destinations. This is especially popular if you are getting married for the second time, or if you don't want to be accompanied by a large family. But since a change in European marriage law a few years ago, marrying in countries such as Italy, Greece and Cyprus has become simpler and is a growing trend. With cheap flights and accommodation, a European wedding can be cost-effective for both you and your guests.

If you are at all unsure about which type of ceremony is right for you, make appointments with your church minister or rabbi and with the local registrar to discuss your options. To check the details of marrying abroad, contact the weddings department of one of the major tour operators.

For a more detailed look at each type of marriage ceremony, see Chapter 5, Your Ceremony, page 64.

It All Starts Here

Buying your ring

Traditionally, the groom-to-be presents his prospective bride with an engagement ring as he goes on bended knee and proposes marriage. It may be a family heirloom or something you have admired on a previous shopping trip; either way, there's something very romantic about being given a ring that he has chosen just for you. But for many couples buying the ring has become a joint decision with the bride-to-be very much involved in choosing the design – you'll be wearing it for many years to come, after all!

The old saying that you should spend three times your average monthly salary on an engagement ring was originally coined by a jewellery company that wanted you to spend as much as possible! But, as with everything else to do with your wedding, you should spend only what you can afford on the engagement ring.

Diamond rings are by far the most popular choice for an engagement ring and are sold according to the four Cs:

Cut The cut determines its brilliance (how sparkly it is!).

Clarity The degree to which the diamond is free from internal flaws. This is what determines the price.

Colour The more colourless the stone the better the quality of the diamond (unless you go for one of the brightly coloured pink, yellow or blue diamonds, which are very pricey).

Carat The weight of the stone, which determines its size. 1 carat is about the size of a small pea. In 1969 Richard Burton gave Elizabeth Taylor a 69-carat diamond, which was the size of a golf ball. Your diamond is likely to be somewhere in between!

Which diamond is right for you?

Round   *Emerald Cut*   *Pear*   *Heart*   *Square*   *Oval*

Diamonds are cut into various shapes and it's important that you try on different styles to see what suits your finger shape and size the best. Platinum has become a popular setting, but gold will never go out of style.

The song has it that diamonds are a girl's best friend – but don't feel you have to choose one for your engagement ring. Royalty has long favoured coloured stones such as emeralds, sapphires and rubies. Or you may prefer to use your birthstone.

Real Bride's Hot Tip
❝ *We're having our wedding on a Friday. It will make a great start to the weekend and has saved us money with most of our suppliers because they weren't busy on that day.* ❞
Samantha Paul, Tunbridge Wells, Kent

Your dream wedding

The first thing you need to think about, probably before you even set the date, is what style of wedding you are going to have. The type of marriage service and the overall size and formality of the day you envisage will all dictate many of your planning choices – certainly the venue, the budget and your outfits, and perhaps even your colour scheme.

Start with a blank piece of paper and write down what's important for your dream wedding. Do you see small and intimate? Big and formal? Or even a beach ceremony somewhere abroad? Is your vision the same as your intended's? Discuss your personal expectations and then take into account the expectations of others, in particular your parents. Ultimately it's your wedding but if forgoing a religious ceremony is likely to spark World War Three, you need to be sure that the aggravation is worth it!

Once you have roughed out your perfect big day, you need to work out whether you can afford to pay for it… but more of that in Chapter 2, Your Budget, page 28. Your next important decision is to set the date for your wedding.

It All Starts Here

13

Setting the date

The most popular time for weddings is between June and September, for the obvious reason that the weather is more reliable! But with the advent of civil weddings in historic buildings, the lure of the candlelit winter wedding has seen a recent rise in couples choosing December and January weddings.

The wedding date and length of your engagement depends on several factors:

Is the venue available? There is no point telling the world when you think you'll be marrying only to discover that your favourite venue is booked. Popular venues get booked up early (often years in advance), particularly from June to September, so you need to move quickly.

Is the registrar available? This is very important if you are planning a civil ceremony at a licensed venue. Don't confirm the location until you know the registrar is free to attend; he or she may well be busy at another wedding at another venue and most local authorities have only two or three registrars.

How long will it take to save up? This is a key consideration if you are paying for a lot of the wedding yourselves. Those extra few months could make all the difference to what you can afford.

Is there a special day for the two of you? Some couples love the romance of marrying on Valentine's Day, on one of their birthdays or on a special anniversary. Marrying on the wedding anniversary of one set of parents is another popular idea.

Can you be flexible? If you have always dreamed of a reception in the sunshine, then a summer wedding is the obvious choice. If you are happy with a wedding inside and the chance of rain isn't an issue, the flexibility on date could save you money because you'll be avoiding the popular 'wedding season'.

Once you've a set the date, it is a good idea to send out 'save-the-date' cards to your guests so they can avoid arranging events of their own that will clash with your big day.

Save the Date

For: Kate and Simon's Wedding
On: Saturday 20th August 2005
At: 2.30pm
In: Cholmondely Hall, Lower Slaughter
Invitation to follow

The guest list

Unless you have an unlimited budget, deciding on the guest list is going to be an exercise in tact and diplomacy. You won't be able to invite everyone you know now or have been friends with in the past, and they can't all bring their other half and their children. So how do you decide who gets the invitation?

Traditionally the guest list is split 50/50 between the bride and her family and the groom and his family. But you need to take other factors into consideration so it is often not as straightforward as that.

Venue size Your venue will dictate how many guests you can have. The standard banqueting suite or hotel ballroom can accommodate 100–150 seated for dinner. If you want anything bigger, your venue options become more limited to very large (and expensive) hotels.

Family size If either or both of you has a large extended family and you need to invite them all, three-quarters of your guest list could be filled before you even think about workmates and friends. This is where compromise may have to come into play. Your parents will want to invite family and, if they are paying the majority of the wedding bill, you are going to have to listen to their wishes.

> ### Real Bride's Hot Tip
> 66 *Don't invite old boyfriends and girlfriends to your wedding – even if you're still friendly. It's a recipe for disaster somewhere along the line.* 99
> **Jessica Druit, Edinburgh**

Your budget Think of each guest as a sum of money; the more guests you invite, the more you have to pay – it's as simple as that. You can definitely think about leaving out the partners of work colleagues and having an adults-only wedding. A pay bar also cuts costs.

Wedding style For many couples, being the focus of attention at a huge wedding sends shivers down the spine. For them, a small, close friends-and-family-only day with a blow-out lunch will appeal far more. It is your day and people will understand if you tell them that is what you would prefer. You can always have a party, without the formality, to celebrate your first month of married life.

The question of children

Whether or not to invite children to your wedding is a difficult one and something you'll have to think about if you are trimming your guest list or you fancy a grown-up big day. Cute kids can make certainly make your wedding photographs but they can also be a pain when they get bored, and weddings are very boring when you're five years old!

If you do decide to invite children, plan some child-friendly aspects into the day. If a lot of under-tens will be joining you, it's a good idea to have a crèche where trained nannies keep the little ones occupied during the pre-dinner drinks and the speeches. Too pricey? You could put all the children on a separate table with their own menu and plenty to keep them amused such as drawing paper, colouring pens and puzzles. If their table has a paper covering, they could be asked to join in making a wonderful coloured picture for the bride and groom to keep.

If you don't want children at your wedding then it's best to make it an adults-only celebration. But you have to mean it. You will risk ruffling a lot of feathers if you allow one or two friends to bring their babies when you have told other friends that the wedding is a child-free day. You will also have to accept that some people won't be able to come because they can't find childcare for the day and evening.

It All Starts Here

Whatever you plan to do, spell it out on the invitation. If children are to be included, put their names on the invitation: if they aren't, just put the parents' names and, when they call to enquire whether their offspring are invited (and they will call), you can politely but firmly explain that your venue/budget dictates that numbers have to be kept to a minimum.

Setting your wedding style

With imagination you can create a wonderful wedding on just about any budget. You want to plan a day that reflects your personalities and for your guests to go away thinking that it was truly 'your day'. Start by going back to your original list of wedding priorities and thinking about the overall style of the wedding you see in your dreams.

Traditional

This is the most popular style of wedding, with a ceremony followed by a drinks reception, a seated meal in the late afternoon/early evening and then a party including dancing to live music or with a DJ.

Pros: You get to spend the whole day with friends and family. It suits both religious and civil ceremonies. **Cons:** It tends to be expensive unless you are doing the catering yourselves.

Informal

This usually involves a civil ceremony followed by a buffet-style reception or cocktail party in the afternoon, with guests departing late afternoon.

Pros: A cost-effective option that will suit the couple who don't want a lot of fuss. **Cons:** You may feel the occasion was all over very quickly (and you would have liked more fuss and attention!).

The wedding weekend

This increasingly popular option involves a select number of guests arriving at a venue on Friday, the wedding taking place during the day on Saturday with a formal reception, then everyone meeting up again on Sunday for breakfast before going home.

Pros: A wonderfully indulgent way of celebrating with friends. **Cons:** Very pricey and, because the type of venue offering this service tends to be smaller country houses, the number of guests you can invite to stay is limited.

The wedding abroad

A good option for couples marrying for the second time, for those with differing religions or for anyone who prefers the minimum of fuss with an endless choice of amazing locations. Choose from destinations as diverse as a Caribbean beach to a palace in Italy.

Pros: A relaxed, informal setting that can be much cheaper than a traditional UK wedding. **Cons:** Some friends and family won't be able to join you due to financial and time constraints.

Give your wedding a theme

Indulge your passions by giving your wedding a very personal theme based around something that interests you or your groom. Use the theme on your stationery and to name each table.

The movies: Name your tables after famous screen lovers, play a silent movie during dinner, put directors' chairs in the cocktail area, or you could even hold the reception in a cinema.

Sport: If you or your man has a sporting passion, think about hiring a sporting venue such as a football ground, racecourse, golf club or bowling alley.

Travel destinations: Name all your tables after places you've visited, or plan to visit as a couple. Paris, Venice and New York sound so much more glamorous than Tables 1, 2 and 3!

Fashion: Probably more one for the girls but for a chic, contemporary feeling naming your tables after fashion designers is fun. Ask your cake maker to bake and decorate piles of handbag-, shoe- and waistcoat-shaped biscuits to have as favours.

Flowers: A floral theme always looks beautiful and works well all year round. If you give each table a flower name, your florist can create a simple centrepiece reflecting that particular bloom.

It All Starts Here

Inspiration through the year

If you're stuck for ideas, the different seasons offer lots of wedding inspiration:

New Year Celebrate New Year's Eve with a wedding. The latest you can actually marry is 6pm, but the party will be in full swing by the time midnight comes. Black tie and ballgowns are the obvious choice for your guests.

Valentine's day Your theme will obviously be hearts, and romance with a capital R. Heart-shaped confetti and invitations, and heart-shaped cookies as favours.

Spring Think fresh colour, growth and renewal. You'll be spoiled for choice with beautiful spring flowers, though spring also means rain so it's probably best not to plan anything outside.

Easter Pastel colours, tea parties and maybe a reception in a conservatory. An Easter egg hunt for the children and splashes of zesty yellow for your colour theme.

Summer The great outdoors beckons at a venue with a terrace or marquee. Put up umbrellas and cover tables with picnic-style tablecloths. String fairy lights in trees and use lanterns when it's dark to maintain the romantic mood.

> ### *Real Bride's Hot Tip*
> *❝ We're having our wedding in Italy. We got the ceremony, weekend accommodation, venue, and food and drink for 50 people for half what we would have paid at home. And the sunshine is just about guaranteed! ❞*
> *Suzie Hunt, Truro, Cornwall*

Autumn Make the most of the autumnal colours by choosing a venue surrounded by parkland. Incorporate reds, bronze and gold into your colour theme.

Winter Cold weather invites you to create a cosy, romantic feeling. Serve hearty dishes accompanied by red wine and ice-cold vodka.

Christmas Celebrate the season with lots of fairy lights, silver balls and red ribbon. Chances are your venue will already be decorated and all you will have to add are your finishing touches.

It All Starts Here

The Bride's Book style quiz

Still undecided about what type of bride you are? Try this quiz to help you decide which style is best for you. It won't give you all the answers, but it might help point you in the right direction.

What is your idea of wedding heaven?

- ❏ a champagne, sit-down dinner, dancing until dawn
- ❏ b a select number of guests dining at your favourite city restaurant
- ❏ c just the two of you somewhere stylish and hot

What is your idea of a dream wedding dress?

- ❏ a tight bodice, big fairytale skirt
- ❏ b slim, slinky and sophisticated
- ❏ c something modern and a little bit sexy

What is your likely wedding colour scheme?

- ❏ a pink, pink and more pink
- ❏ b lots of classic white, perhaps teamed with a splash of colour
- ❏ c you weren't really thinking about having a colour scheme

Which bouquet appeals to you the most?

- ❏ a old-fashioned pink roses
- ❏ b lily-of-the-valley
- ❏ c you would prefer a Lulu Guinness handbag to a bouquet

What would be your ideal mode of wedding transport?

- ❏ a a Cinderella-style coach and horses
- ❏ b a white Rolls Royce
- ❏ c a self-drive sports car

What is your dream honeymoon?

- ❏ a a Caribbean island
- ❏ b Venice
- ❏ c Miami

Who are your favourite celebrity bride and groom?

❏ a Victoria and David Beckham
❏ b Catherine Zeta Jones and Michael Douglas
❏ c Jordan and Peter Andre

You scored mostly As

Miss Romantic You just love the whole idea of getting married and have probably been dreaming about your big day since you were a little girl. Just don't forget that Prince Charming needs to play a part in his own wedding; you'll need to come off cloud nine occasionally to avoid pre-wedding tension.

Style tips Hearts, cupids and fairies will probably adorn everything from the invitations to your place settings. Old-fashioned roses in pink or white will appeal to your romantic nature and releasing white doves at the end of the ceremony is a stylish touch that will guarantee the 'ahh' factor from your guests.

You scored mostly Bs

Miss Sophisticated You were probably the little girl who was always dressing up in her mum's high heels. You like the finer things in life and you are secretly nostalgic for the days of movie-star glamour epitomised by Grace Kelly and Audrey Hepburn.

Style tips Your wedding style is classically elegant, with a nod in the direction of modern chic. You will probably want to hold your reception in a stylish townhouse hotel or a marquee in the country. Every detail will be considered and your guests will know that your perfectionist hand has been involved in everything.

You scored mostly Cs

Miss Trendy You are known as the life and soul of the party and some of your friends are probably surprised you are getting married at all – much too traditional for you! You are endlessly creative and you love colour but you can be disorganised so employing a wedding planner may be a good investment to get the job done.

Style tips Your guests will love your originality and sense of fun. How about food stalls offering a variety of nibbles from sushi to mini hot dogs? Entertain everyone with roving magicians performing close-up magic and then get the party started with the latest hits played by the hottest DJ.

66 *Every wedding detail will be defined by your own personal style.* **99**

Seasonal style and colour

The well co-ordinated wedding will always have a theme of some kind – a harmony of style, colour and mood that will delight your guests from the minute they walk through the door and make you feel extra special too.

Setting a theme may sound a little formal but it doesn't have to be theatrical; it can be as straightforward as choosing one particular colour scheme. Be guided by what you like and by the time of year you are marrying. There's no point in dreaming of peonies and strawberries if you are getting married in February: likewise, if the lure of candlelight and open fires is a must, a summer wedding is not for you.

The spring wedding

The look Spring colour themes range from bright and sunny to a subdued palette of pinks, lilac and greens. The weather is pretty changeable so you are likely to be celebrating indoors. Make the most of the lighter evenings by choosing a venue with lots of windows.

The flowers For an informal look, choose flowers with a soft shape such as sweet peas and put them in mini buckets on each table. For a more formal centrepiece, lilies or tulips are plentiful at this time of year and available in a myriad of bright colours. A single stem tied with a name tag makes a pretty place card.

Food and drink A favourite idea for a spring wedding, particularly around Easter, is to host an afternoon tea party with sandwiches, decorated biscuits and cupcakes piled high on old-fashioned cake stands. Serve a mixture of unusual teas as well as lashings of pink champagne. For a sit-down meal, take advantage of the season; piles of seasonal vegetables and spring lamb makes a delicious main course.

The summer wedding

The look White or pastels will always look cool on a warm, sunny day. Choose fabrics such as organza or voile that flutter in the breeze, and put up oversize white umbrellas for welcome shade. You can't guarantee the weather so eating outside might not be an option; a conservatory with doors you can open is one solution, or a marquee with open sides to let in the evening air but at the same time to provide cover is another. Decorate any outside area with strings of fairy lights or put lanterns in the trees to keep the party going as darkness descends.

The flowers Ask your florist about the best hot-weather blooms that are less likely to wilt in the heat. Sunflowers will add an amazing splash of colour at a country wedding, and you can never go wrong with all-white flower arrangements; tightly packed centrepieces of old-fashioned white roses or huge armfuls of airy gypsophila looks beautiful.

Food and drink Keep canapés light and serve them from trays of ice to prevent anything becoming sweaty in the heat. Your guests won't want anything too heavy – salmon is always a good choice, served with interesting salads and new potatoes. Think about setting up old-fashioned stalls on a patio serving freshly made lemonade (with a splash of gin or vodka if preferred!) and an ice-cream stall.

The autumn wedding

The look Make the most of the season and incorporate all the amazing autumnal hues into your colour scheme. You don't have to go too 'harvest festival' with the whole look; a glorious rich aubergine, silky russet and every shade of gold work equally well at this time of the year. The evenings will be drawing in so, if your venue allows it, make candlelight a big part of the decoration. Tealights are very versatile and an inexpensive (and safe) way to add a romantic glow to any room.

The flowers Think fiery colours for your bouquet and reception arrangements. Gerbera, euphorbia, dahlias and calla lilies will all be plentiful, as will some amazing foliage and autumnal berries that you can use to great effect.

Food and drink Your guests will appreciate warming food and you may like to try more intense flavours with hints of delicious ginger and cinnamon. If you are looking to do something different, how about setting up food stalls offering different tastes from around the world? Everything from sushi to hot dogs, Chinese nibbles to mini Yorkshire puddings – all served buffet-style – allowing guests to indulge their taste buds to the full.

The winter wedding

The look You have two main choices with a winter wedding, either rich and sumptuous red, greens and gold or, for a more contemporary look, ice white. If your wedding is near Christmas, the venue may well already be decked out with Christmas trees and decorations so you'll be half-way there. Christmas decorations, bought in bulk, are wonderfully versatile and can be heaped into inexpensive glass containers for decoration and hung from silver-sprayed twigs. The days will be short, so use lots of candlelight and fairy lights (much more attractive than overhead lighting).

The flowers What could be more beautiful than deep red, velvety roses surrounded by lush greenery? Ask your florist about creating a couple of theatrical arrangements to stand on each side of the entrance to the dining area, overflowing with foliage and berries. For a less formal look, white roses, camellias and potted amaryllis are stunning.

Food and drink Try mulled wine, hot toddies and hearty canapés to welcome your guests from the cold, then treat them to a feast of flavours as everyone tends to feel hungrier when it is chilly. Think about pumpkin or potato soup, followed by roast beef or game served with traditional vegetables. Finish with a comforting dessert such as treacle tart or sticky toffee pudding with lashings of cream.

Colour combinations

Successful colour combinations that work for any style of wedding.

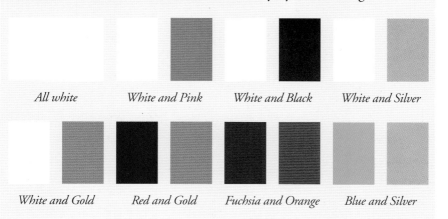

All white	*White and Pink*	*White and Black*	*White and Silver*
White and Gold	*Red and Gold*	*Fuchsia and Orange*	*Blue and Silver*

Suzannah Hastie &
Andrew Stanton

Leez Priory, Essex

Menu

Chapter 2

Your Budget

There's no doubt about it, weddings are expensive. But you don't have to go into debt to have an amazing big day. Memorable weddings are not about how much you spend; with some clever planning you can make any budget work, big or small.

First things first. Sit down with your fiancé and work out what kind of wedding you want. Write down everything that is important to you both – the style of venue, how many guests you want to invite, the dress, the honeymoon… whatever you think matters to make your day truly special. Try to write everything in order of priority. If a designer dress or a Caribbean honeymoon is at the top of the list, that's fine. It just means you may not be able to have vintage champagne or serve filet of beef to your guests at the reception.

Split the list into two columns, the first is all the essentials (officiant's fees, the venue, food and drink) the second is optionals (video, limo, string quartet for the ceremony) that you could live without. Compare your list with that of your fiancé to make sure you are both in agreement, then agree to compromise on any areas where you don't see eye-to-eye.

Now work out your potential wedding budget. Come up with a figure that is based on your savings, what you think you'll be able to save during your engagement, and any contributions you believe will be coming your way from both sets of parents. This should give you an idea of the total you have to spend.

To see how your budget may then be spent, try using this simple formula as a guide to what is typically spent on each area:

Reception, including food and drink .... 40 per cent
Venue/ceremony/musicians .... 15 per cent
Outfits .... 10 per cent
Flowers/entertainment/transport .... 10 per cent
Photography/video .... 7 per cent
Stationery.. 3 per cent
Honeymoon .... 10 per cent
Miscellaneous/unexpected extras .... 5 per cent

The UK national average wedding budget for 2006, based on an annual survey conducted by *You & Your Wedding* magazine, is just over £20,000. You can of course get married for a lot less, but this figure does give you an idea of what real couples are spending on their wedding.

Once you have divided your budget according to the formula, you can see what you have available to spend across the various sectors. Scary isn't it? What seemed like a decent total budget when you started probably doesn't look very much now you have split it up. But don't panic! You haven't really started shopping yet and there are lots of ways to make your money go further.

Family contributions

In days gone by it was expected that the father of the bride pretty much paid for everything. But not any more; the modern wedding is very much a family affair, with many couples paying for the majority of the expenses using their own money, though often with contributions from both sets of parents.

It's advisable to have the money conversation with your parents early on in your planning process. There's no point in making assumptions about what they may or may not be willing to give you, and you certainly don't want to base your budget on money that may not be available.

Be sensitive to your parents' financial situation and don't expect them to empty their savings account for your wedding. If you know money is tight they can always contribute their organisational skills. Maybe your mum could make the cake, your dad could help with reading over supplier contacts, and both of them could offer advice at menu and wine tastings and come to view potential venues.

If either set of parents does want to pay for a large part of the wedding, lucky you! Just be sure that they don't think their financial clout means that they now have a bigger say in the style of the day and more control over the guest list. It can be very difficult to tell your parents you would rather invite workmates in preference to distant relatives or childhood neighbours if you are using their money.

One solution is to allocate parents' contributions for specified areas. For example, the bride's parents' money pays for the food; the groom's parents' money pays for the flowers and the drinks. This way they'll feel that they have paid for something specific but not feel they have overall control.

Once you know how much is going into the wedding fund, it's a good idea to set up a separate 'wedding bank account', which will finance everything to do with the wedding. This way you can easily track what you are spending without the money getting muddled with general household and personal expenses. You can also see how much is left.

Real Bride's Hot Tip
66*Register at www. youandyourwedding. co.uk and use the online budgeter. You put in your total and it splits it across the expenses. It then gets updated and revised as you spend. You can also print it out.*99
Claire Sutton, Surrey

Going solo

Lots of couples choose to pay for their own wedding and it's the best way to ensure you have everything your way; but it also means you have to find all the money. So where do you begin?

Start saving as soon as possible

10–20 per cent of every pay packet should be your aim. Try instigating a few cost-cutting measures such as taking a packed lunch to work, staying in with friends rather than eating out and delaying major purchases and weekends away until after the wedding. It's amazing how small savings can add up to a decent chunk of cash at the end of every month.

Open a wedding account

Whether or not you are getting contributions, a separate account is a good idea and makes tracking the wedding finances straightforward.

Be savings wise

One of you may earn considerably more than the other or have more debts, so be upfront from the start about how much you can afford to contribute. Then speak to a financial adviser about the best way for your wedding fund to earn interest. If you are having a long engagement and not spending for a few months, get the money earning for you.

Do it yourself

Where possible, do things yourself rather than employing someone to do it for you: ask a computer-savvy friend to design your invitations and make the seating plan; have a girly evening with your best friends making simple favours; check out ebay (www.ebay.co.uk) for wedding bargains; and look out for sample sales at the local wedding dress shop.

Compromise, compromise

Okay, so your dream wedding day just isn't happening on your allocated budget and winning the lottery seems unlikely. What are you going to do?

You could, of course, take out a loan to boost your budget. Sensibly planned and with advice from your bank, this is a viable option – providing you can pay the money back without giving up eating, drinking and socialising for the first two years of married life!

Putting any of your wedding expenses on to a credit card is a recipe for misery; credit card companies charge a lot for the privilege and, unless you know you can pay off the balance quickly, it's the most expensive way of borrowing money.

But before you rush to increase the size of your budget, how about taking a good hard look at what you want to spend to see if there are areas for compromise? All but the most lavish weddings are an exercise in compromise somewhere.

The reception takes up the biggest slice of the wedding budget, so start with this.

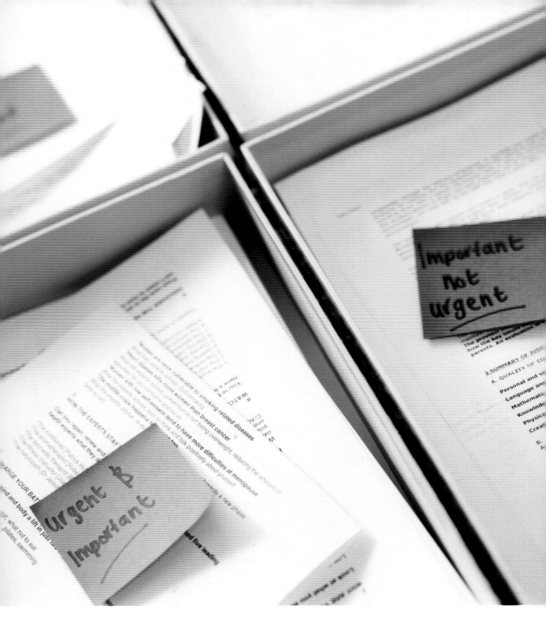

And since the amount you spend is directly in line with how many guests you are inviting, take a long, hard look at the proposed guest list.

- Do all your distant relatives need an invitation?
- Are all your old school friends still that important to you?
- Must you invite your workmate's partner (whom you may never have met)?
- Does every member of your fiancé's rugby team need to be invited?
- Should you invite children or could you get away with an adults-only event?

You don't want to appear mean, but every guest you invite is going to cost you money, so make sure having them with you as you celebrate your special day actually matters.

Evening-only guests

Some couples cut reception costs by inviting one set of friends to the main part of the day, and then have a second 'b-list' coming along in the evening. Whether or not this appeals will depend on your own circumstances; my feeling is that if they aren't close enough friends to come to see you exchange your vows – and after all, that's what the day is all about – then you don't really need to invite them. A second reception with even limited food and drink still adds to your budget.

Creative cost-cutting

The secret to creative wedding budgeting is to choose areas where your guests are unlikely to notice that you are cost-cutting.

A shorter day The longer your guests are with you, the more you have to spend on food, drink and entertainment, so shorten the wedding day. Ask for a late-afternoon ceremony slot so there's less time to fill between it and the sit-down reception that follows.

A weekday wedding Avoiding popular (and expensive) weekends will save you money. Venues and suppliers are much more likely to offer you a good deal on less popular days. A Friday wedding will be viewed by many of your guests as a lovely start to the weekend.

Buffet v formal sit-down Seating all your guests and serving each course is the most expensive option because of the number of waiting staff involved, so a buffet can make financial sense. Just make sure it suits your style of event. Buffets aren't always the best option if you have a lot of older and younger guests who will find queuing and carrying plates tricky.

A-list cocktails If dancing into the night isn't your thing, invite your guests to a stylish cocktail party with lots of finger food and interesting drinks. Or how about an afternoon tea party with mini sandwiches, cute cupcakes and pink champagne? A shorter, stylish event will delight most guests. Just make it clear on the invitation what you are planning and that the wedding will be ending at a set time.

Less is more Decorating the ceremony and reception venues can be very costly, especially if you want to use a lot of flowers. Ask your florist about using less expensive foliage and perhaps creating one or two eye-catching arrangements that, strategically placed, will impress your guests and do away with the need for individual arrangements on every table. You could also save money by moving any large arrangements from the ceremony to the reception venue while the photographs are being taken.

No surprises

It's a good idea to set aside at least 5 per cent, and preferably 10 per cent, of your budget for unexpected extras because something will definitely come up that you hadn't budgeted for. Areas you may not have accounted for include:

Tips 10 per cent of the food and drinks bill for the caterer to divide among the staff. £5–20 for musicians, bar staff, cloakroom attendants, DJs and delivery drivers quickly adds up to a substantial amount.

Dress alterations You may lose a few pounds so the dress needs taking in. You may decide something isn't quite right and must be altered. It will all add towards the final bill.

Postage Lots of couples forget they have to post their invitations and then copies of the gift list as this gets requested.

Corkage If you are taking your own wines rather than using the venue's, you may be charged a corkage fee for chilling, opening and serving – and this can be anything up to £10 per bottle, which adds considerably to your drinks bill.

Overtime The party is in full swing and an extra hour of music would be fantastic. Just remember that the band will charge you for the privilege (maybe double time after midnight).

If the budget goes out of control

Despite all your best efforts, you are half-way through the planning process but your wedding fund is disappearing fast and there is still masses of important things you need to buy. What are you going to do?

First of all, don't panic. Sit down with your fiancé and go through everything that has been booked to see where savings can be made. This is where that priority list mentioned at the start of the chapter comes into play. To avoid starting married life with a huge debt – and there's nothing romantic about having no money – you must compromise.

Ask your suppliers for their suggestions on how you can save money. They are experts and will have worked on all kinds of weddings with all sizes of budget. It may be that you need to choose a cheaper main course or less expensive wine. The flower budget may need to be cut, and do you really need to give all your guests a favour? Entertainment can be expensive and none of your guests will mind listening to a compilation of your favourite music played on CD rather than hearing a live band as they eat their meal.

Work through every part of the big day schedule and ask yourself the same question: do we really need this? If you don't, then cut it out.

Real Bride's Hot Tip
❝Have the photographer only at the ceremony. For lots of informal shots of the reception put a couple of disposable cameras on each table for guests to use and then collect them up at the end of the evening.❞
Sue Gallagher, Birmingham

Once you have made your cost-cutting decisions, stick to them. And just remember when you see yet another gorgeous little 'must have' in the latest wedding magazine, your guests are coming to celebrate your marriage. Ask them in a month's time what they ate, what the favours were and what colour the napkins were. They won't remember. What they will remember is your happy smiling faces. Job done!

Natalie Evans &
Dino Mussell

Babington House,
Somerset

Chapter *3*

Your Venue

Castle or country house, hotel or the local village hall? The possibilities are almost endless and choosing the perfect location is one of your key planning tasks. With the hottest venues getting snapped up quickly, you'd better start your search now!

Your venue is the backdrop to your wedding so you will want to find the perfect location. But where do you start? The type of building you look for will depend on whether or not you are having a religous or a civil ceremony. If you are having a religious ceremony, you will need to find a reception venue within about twenty minutes' drive of the church or synagogue: if you are having a civil ceremony, you either need a reception venue within easy reach of the register office or to choose a licensed building where you can hold both the ceremony and the reception.

Since 1994, a change in the law has meant that couples in England, Northern Ireland and Wales can marry in any building with a marriage licence. The local registrar travels to your chosen venue and performs the marriage ceremony. At present there are over 3,000 licensed properties and these range from castles and stately homes to hotels, sporting venues, art galleries and museums. To comply with the law, the building granted the licence must be a permanent structure. So you can't get married in the open air, for example in the garden of a hotel, even if the venue holds a marriage licence. To obtain a list of licensed venues in your area, contact the local authority or log on to www.ons.gov.uk where you can request a print-out of every licensed building in the country for a small fee.

Starting your search

You may have a favourite venue in mind or you may have no idea at all. Either way, it's a good idea to do some research to find out just what is available.

Online www.youandyourwedding.co.uk has a handy online venue search facility that lists all the licensed venues in a particular county, with contact details.

Yellow Pages This is very useful if you are looking for a reception venue that doesn't have to have a marriage licence. Look in the listings for banqueting, clubs, halls, hotels, restaurants and room hire. The back section of magazines such as *You & Your Wedding* and *Cosmopolitan Bride* will have a wealth of classified ads for lots of different venues. Magazines also do regular features reviewing different styles of venue which can be very useful.

Recommendation Nothing beats personal recommendation, so do ask recently married friends about their venue – what they liked and what they didn't. Other suppliers such as your photographer and florist will also have worked at lots of different places and will be a good source of inspiration.

Once you have drawn up a shortlist of places that warrant further investigation, give each of them a call before arranging a visit and request details of what facilities it can provide. There's not much point in viewing a venue that looks great on the outside but can only seat 80 guests for dinner when you need space for 120. Your initial calls need to make sure that all the basic boxes are ticked before you visit. If a potential venue has a website, pay attention to whether it has a designated section for weddings. While it isn't essential that a venue regularly hosts wedding parties, it's advantageous if it is used to this type of event and its staff should be able to recommend suppliers such as caterers, photographers and florists – all of which will make your life easier. Having looked through each venue's literature to see what it can offer, you are ready to make some viewing appointments.

> ### *Real Bride's Hot Tip*
> 66 *You'll know when you've found the perfect venue. It's not just the building, it's the people too. You need to like and trust the manager and wedding co-ordinator – your big day is in their hands!* 99
> *Carey Lovett,*
> *Buckinghamshire*

What makes a perfect venue?

Before visiting any potential venue, arm yourself with a list of key questions. It's too easy to get distracted by a wow! garden or a beautiful terrace and forget the practical things such as car parking.

The rooms

If you are looking for premises with a civil licence you'll be shown during your tour the specific rooms that are licensed for marriage. In large venues there may be several rooms to choose from: in smaller venues just one room. You'll also be shown suitable rooms for a drinks reception, the sit-down part of the day and for dancing. If the weather is likely to be good, ask to see any patio or gardens which are available for use as well.

Try to imagine how each room will feel with your proposed number of guests. It needs to be big enough, but not so big that it feels as though half your guests haven't shown up. If you are planning a summer wedding, take a good look at any outside areas that may be available to you. Is there room to erect a marquee in the gardens? This is an obvious solution for the venue that's tight on space inside.

Exclusive use

Larger venues will sometimes hold more than one wedding on the same date and if privacy is important to you make sure you check whether this is a possibility. Arranging for exclusive use of a venue will come at a price but it may be worth it to avoid queuing with someone else's guests for the toilets and listening to their disco as the evening progresses.

The cost

Hiring the venue is a big part of your wedding budget so, before booking anything, make sure you get the maths right. Most venues charge a flat hire fee, though some may charge by the hour. Smaller venues will give you exclusive use for a set amount of time (usually 24 hours): larger venues will work out a fee based on the number of rooms you are using and for how long. Most venues can provide a per head package price depending on the number of guests and what you eat. This will usually include the cost of the tables, chairs, set menu and set amount of drink to accompany the meal. All of this should be specified in their literature and you will need to read through the small print at home.

On-site wedding co-ordinator

Most large venues have a wedding organiser on their staff who will be your main contact during the run-up to the big day and also be present on the day to ensure that everything runs smoothly. At smaller venues you are likely to be dealing with the venue manager. It's important that you like – and trust – this person since he or she will be your main contact and the one who interprets your ideas and makes them happen. If you don't feel an affinity with this person, it probably isn't the right venue for you.

The lighting

Lighting can make or break the whole mood of your wedding. If you are marrying during the day, you should choose a reception room with plenty of windows. Who wants to spend hours in a poorly lit room when it's sunny outside? For evening and winter weddings you will want to be able to control the lighting. Dim is not good – but neither are harsh strip lights more suited to a conference. Candlelight is always a possibility but ask first; many historic venues do not allow naked flames. Try to visit the venue at the same time of day you will be holding your wedding, or when light conditions will be similar, so you can see how it will look.

Real Bride's Hot Tip

"For an informal wedding, how about hiring a photographer's studio? They're often a big white space with lots of windows and need minimal decoration to look trendy."

Suzanne Clark, London

The colour scheme

If you have your heart set on a particular colour theme, the venue decoration needs to at least complement your chosen colours. A pastel theme would be overpowered by a red and gold room. Accept there's nothing you can do about carpets and wall coverings and move on to the next venue.

The nitty-gritty

Your initial visit is also the time to check all the little details: Is the venue clean and tidy? Are there any noise or time restrictions? Are the toilet facilities and car parking adequate? Are the gardens child-friendly (ponds and swimming pools must be safe)? Is there accommodation or at least changing facilities for the main

bridal party? Also check whether you have to use the venue's preferred suppliers or whether you are free to bring in your own caterers.

Do it yourself

If you are on a budget, hiring a village hall or a function room is a good option. Just make sure you aren't taking on too much. This type of venue means providing your own catering, hiring all the furniture, linens, glasses and cutlery, putting up some sort of room decoration – and then clearing it all up afterwards. The same goes for holding a reception at home. Unless you, or your parents, have a very spacious home and gardens this can be a major undertaking. A marquee in your childhood home is a lovely idea but involves a lot of upheaval and hard work.

Your dream venue

So you've found the place you want to celebrate your marriage in. It ticks all the boxes for location, service and atmosphere. So what now? Expect to pay a 10–15 per cent deposit to secure your chosen date. The venue should then send you a contract, which you need to check very carefully to make sure it includes everything you discussed and that no hidden extras have appeared.

Your dream venue should be somewhere that feels as individual as the two of you

The written contract should include the following

✔ the total cost and a detailed breakdown of what is included

✔ the deposit and when it was paid

✔ the balance to be paid and when this is due

✔ the date and time of the wedding

✔ the exact rooms where the ceremony, drinks, dining and dancing will be held

✔ a complete list of what is provided – tables, chairs, linens, cutlery etc.

✔ the name and contact details for the wedding organiser or venue manager

✔ the cancellation and refund policy

✔ anything else you agreed at your first meetings

Take time to check all contract details, asking someone else, such as your parents, to double check everything. Then once you have signed, keep a copy of the contract safe in your wedding folder for easy reference and to check any details as your plans progress.

Questions to ask your venue

Is it available on our proposed wedding date?

How much does it cost?

Does it have all-inclusive packages?

Is there an on-site wedding co-ordinator?

Is there suitable overnight accommodation?

Does it have liability insurance?

Will we have exclusive use of the venue?

Can we use all the facilities or only certain rooms/areas?

Can we use the gardens? Can we erect a marquee?

Do we have to pay a deposit?

Are all tables, chairs, cutlery and linens included in the price?

Does it have in-house catering?

Can we bring our own caterer?

Is there a bar? If not, does the venue have a drinks licence?

Are there any restrictions on noise or the time the reception has to end?

Is there enough car parking for the proposed number of guests?

Can we change any of the décor?

Can we move any pictures or furniture?

What is the cancellation policy?

Fantastic wedding venues

There are literally thousands of wonderful places to hold a wedding but here is just a selection of my personal favourites around Britain.

Hotels

Angel Hotel, Midhurst, Sussex
01730 812421
www.theangelmidhurst.co.uk

Babington House, Frome, Somerset
01373 812266
www.babingtonhouse.co.uk

Baliffscourt Hotel, Climping, Sussex
01903 723 511
www.hshotels.co.uk

Bodysgallen Hall, Llandudno, Wales
01494 584 466
www.bodysgallen.com

Chewton Glen, New Milton, Hampshire
01425 275341
www.chewtonglen.com

Claridge's Hotel, London (photograph below)
020 7629 8860
www.claridges.co.uk

Devonshire Arms, Skipton, Yorkshire
01756 718111
www.devonshirehotels.co.uk

The Dorchester, London
020 7629 8888
www.thedorchester.co.uk

The Lanesborough, London
020 7259 5599
www.lanesborough.co.uk

The Lowry, Manchester
0161 827 4000
www.thelowry.com

Lugger Hotel, Truro, Cornwall
01872 501322
www.luggerhotel.com

Le Manoir Aux Quat' Saisons, Great Milton, Oxfordshire
01844 278881
www.manoir.com

Priory Bay, Seaview, Isle of Wight
01983 613146
www.priorybay.co.uk

The Ritz, London
020 7493 8181
www.theritzlondon.co.uk

The Samling, Windermere
01539 431922
www.thesamling.com

The Savoy, London
020 7836 4343
www.savoy-group.co.uk

Seaham Hall, Seaham, Co Durham
0191 516 1441
www.seaham-hall.com

St David's Hotel, Cardiff
029 2045 4045
www.thestdavidshotel.com

Stapleford Park, Melton Mowbray
01572 787522
www.stapleford.co.uk

Tresanton, St Mawes, Cornwall
01326 270055
www.tresanton.com

The Victoria at Holkham, Norfolk
01328 711008
www.holkham..co.uk

Wyck Hill House Hotel, Stow on the Wold, Gloucestershire
01451 831936
www.wrensgroup.com

Historic houses
and stately homes

Alexandra Palace
020 8365 4141
www.alexandrapalace.co.uk

Amberley Castle, Arundel, Sussex
01798 831992
www.amberleycastle.co.uk

Blenheim Palace, Woodstock, Gloucestershire
01993 8119091
www.blenheimpalace.com

Chiswick House, London
020 8995 0508
www.english-heritage.org.uk

Crewe Hall, Crewe
01270 2533333
www.crewehall.com

Eltham Palace, London
020 8294 2548
www.elthampalace.co.uk

Fountains Abbey, Ripon, Yorkshire
01765 608888
www.nationaltrust.org.uk

Hampton Court Palace, Surrey
0870 751 5175
www.hrp.org.uk

Highclere Castle, Newbury, Berkshire (photograph above)
01635 253210
www.highclerecastle.co.uk

Holbeck Ghyll, Windermere
015394 32375
www.holbeckghyll.com

Leeds Castle, Kent
01622 765400
www.leeds-castle.com

Longleat, Warminster, Wiltshire
01985 844400
www.longleat.co.uk

Osterley Park, London
020 8232 5050
www.nationaltrust.org.uk

Penshurst Place, Tonbridge, Kent
01892 870307
www.penshurstplace.com

Somerlyton Hall and Gardens, Lowestoft, Suffolk (photograph above)
01502 730224
www.somerlyton.co.uk

Sunningdale Park, Ascot, Berkshire
01344 634391
www.initialstyle.co.uk

Syon Park, London
020 8758 1888
www.syonpark.co.uk

Tatton Park, Cheshire
01625 534405
www.tattonpark.org.uk

The Vyne, Basingstoke, Hampshire
01256 883858
www.nationaltrust.org.uk

Woburn Abbey, Woburn, Bedfordshire
01525 290666
www.woburnabbey.co.uk

Unusual venues

Blackpool Tower Ballroom
01253 622242
www.theblackpooltower.co.uk/ballroom

Chelsea Physic Garden, London
020 7353 5646
www.chelseaphysicgarden.co.uk

Gondola, Grasmere
015394 41288
www.nationaltrust.org.uk

Larmar Tree Gardens, Salisbury, Wiltshire
01725 516971
www.larmartreegardens.co.uk

The London Eye, London
0870 2202223
www.londoneye.com

National Railway Museum, York
01904 621261
www.nrm.ac.uk

Natural History Museum, London
020 7942 5000
www.nhm.ac.uk

Pinewood Studios, Iver, Buckinghamshire
01753 651126
www.pinewoodshepperton.com

Portmeirion, Gwynedd, Wales
01766 770000
www.portmeirion.wales.com

Pump Room and Roman Baths, Bath
01225 477782
www.romanbaths.co.uk

The Royal Pavilion, Brighton
01273 292815
www.royalpavilion.brighton.co.uk

Romantic venues

Althorp, Althorp, Nothampton
01604 772103
www.althorp.com

Armathwaite Hall, Keswick, Cumbria
017687 76551
www.armathwaite-hall.com

Atholl Palace, Perthshire
01796 472400
www.athollpalace.com

Belvoir Castle, Near Grantham, Leicestershire
01476 871001
www.belvoircastle.com

Bovey Castle, Dartmoor, Devon (photograph right)
01647 44005
www.boveycastle.com

Drumtochty Castle, Scotland
01561 320169
www.drumtochtyunlimited.com

Hedingham Castle, Halstead, Essex
01787 460261
www.headinghamcastle.co.uk

Kew Gardens, London
0870 7815075
www.kew.org

Leez Priory, Chelmsford, Essex
01245 361555
www.leezpriory.co.uk

The Lords of the Manor, Upper Slaughter, Gloucestershire
01451 820243
www.lordsofthemanor.com

The Matara Centre, Kingscote, Gloucestershire
01453 861050
www.matara.co.uk

Rudding Park, Harrogate, Yorkshire
01423 871050
www.ruddingpark.com

Stoke Park, Stoke Poges, Buckinghamshire
01753 717171
www.stokeparkclub.com

The Walled Gardens at Ellingham, Ringwood, Hampshire
01425 480819
www.ellinghamgarden.co.uk

Your Venue

*Kerry Loughlin
& Ben Webb*

Syon Park, Middlesex

Chapter 4

Roles and Responsibilities

A wedding is all about teamwork, getting together a network of people to support you throughout your engagement and on the big day. There's plenty to be done and the good news is there's a role for just about everyone who wants to be involved.

Weddings are a lot of hard work and you are going to need some help to make sure everything runs smoothly, particularly if you work full time. I'm assuming that your groom is playing a big part in his own wedding, supporting you and helping to make key decisions every step of the way. But, before giving anyone else a big part to play in your day, take a minute to familiarise yourself with what will be expected of each role. Not all of your nearest and dearest will be suited to a spot in the limelight.

The chief bridesmaid

A chief bridesmaid who is already married is also known as the matron of honour. Traditionally this role is given to your sister or best friend but there is no reason why it can't be your mum or even a close male friend. It is an important role, not only helping with the organisation but also providing moral support and (probably) a shoulder to cry on through the many ups and down of the planning process. Being chief bridesmaid is not for everyone so don't be offended if you ask someone but get turned down. It's not everyone's idea of fun to be a central player on the stage at a big event and your best friend may be more suited to a role away from the spotlight, for example handling the invitation RSVP list. It doesn't mean she doesn't want to be involved or loves you any less.

Once you have chosen your best girl, and she has said yes, don't presume she'll know what to do. It's up to you to outline everything you want done and when you need it to be done.

The chief bridesmaid's duties

Her specific wedding duties include the following:

- Supporting the bride at all times as she plans her dream wedding – listening to the moans, mopping up the tears and generally being there whenever and wherever she needs you.
- Helping to keep track of guest list RSVPs, writing envelopes, spreading the word about where the gift list is registered, making favours, baking cookies… just about anything that needs to be done.
- Acting as shopping partner when you are buying the wedding dress, and helping to choose the bridesmaids' outfits.
- Organising a suitable hen night; getting together the group of invitees and taking care of any accommodation, deposits, transportation etc.
- Making sure all the other bridesmaids have sorted out their dresses and accessories.
- Making sure all the other bridesmaids are aware of any duties, have made hair and make-up arrangements and are up to speed with all the timings for the big day.
- Helping the bride to dress on the morning of the wedding. Ensuring all the other bridesmaids are presentable and ready on time.
- Leaving for the ceremony with the bride's mother and other bridesmaids.
- Walking down the aisle before or behind the bride, whichever the bride decides she prefers.

> ### Real Bride's Hot Tip
> **❝I really couldn't choose between my sister and my best friend – one of them would have to be disappointed – so I had two chief bridesmaids. I split the role equally and it worked out brilliantly.❞**
> *Stacy Lomax, Cardiff*

- Lifting up and rearranging the bride's veil at the altar. Holding her bouquet and her gloves, if she is wearing any, during the ceremony.
- Giving a reading, if required. Signing the register as one of the witnesses.
- Ensuring the bride and all the bridesmaids look presentable for the photographs (it is a good idea to give a friend who isn't one of the maids a small bag containing hairpins, hairspray, safety pins, plasters etc. for emergency touch-ups).
- Standing in the receiving line, if there is one.
- Mingling with the guests, making sure everyone has someone to talk to and nobody is feeling left out.
- Sitting at the top table throughout the meal.
- If it is a buffet reception, it will be helpful for the bride if you get her something to eat. The happy couple often miss out on most of the menu because they are so busy talking to their guests.
- Dancing with the best man, the groom and the father of the bride.
- Helping to smooth over any potential guest fallings-out as far as possible, ideally before the bride or groom become aware of them.
- If the bride is changing into a going-away outfit, helping her get ready.
- Arranging for the wedding dress and any gifts received at the reception to be transported and stored safely until after the honeymoon.

The best man

The choice of best man probably causes the bride more sleepless nights than it does the groom! If you are worried that your groom is going to choose someone you feel is totally wrong for such responsibility, my advice would be to tread carefully. It's up to your groom to choose his right-hand man and this will usually be his brother or best friend. For you to start rubbishing his friend's abilities before he has even been asked is liable to cause huge offence. Anyway, the chances are you will be pleasantly surprised. Weddings bring out the best in people; yes, even that hard-drinking, joke-telling fool you put up with every Saturday night at the rugby club is likely to be transformed if given the role of best man!

The best man's duties

His specific wedding duties include the following:

- Helping the groom to buy or rent his outfit. Arranging for fathers and ushers to rent their outfits in plenty of time.
- Arranging a suitable stag do, at least two weeks before the wedding; co-ordinating accommodation, any deposits, timings and transportation.
- Spending the night before the wedding with the groom. Making sure he gets ready in plenty of time. Travelling with the groom to the ceremony venue, aiming to arrive at least 15 minutes before the bride.
- Making sure the ushers know what they have to do and where they should be standing at the ceremony.
- Standing next to the groom at the altar while he waits for his bride.
- Keeping the wedding rings safe until they are needed.
- Give a reading, if required. Signing the register as one of the witnesses.
- Paying the officiant's fee after the ceremony is over. Paying the choir, organist etc. if necessary.
- Making sure the photographer takes shots of all the key family members and guests before the reception.
- Standing in the receiving line at the reception, if there is one.
- Mingling with guests, ensuring everyone is included and nobody is left out.
- Sitting at the top table during the meal.
- Giving a speech after the bride's father and the groom have delivered theirs.
- Dancing with the chief bridesmaid, the bride and both mothers.
- If the couple are leaving the reception for another hotel or going to the airport, making sure transport is booked or their car is waiting, and filled with fuel. A little light car decoration will be appreciated: anything over-the-top will not.
- Arranging for the groom's suit to be taken from the venue and stored safely or returned to the hire shop.

Real Bride's Hot Tip

His best mate was my idea of a nightmare best man. But on the day he was great. I couldn't fault him and his speech was touching rather than crude. My tip would be to trust your man's instinct!

Sally Curtis, Maidstone

The bridesmaids

How many bridesmaids you have is up to you and, to a certain extent, the style and formality of the wedding. Usually the bigger and more formal the wedding, the more attendants you have. Bridesmaids can be relatives or friends, old or young. But, before asking anyone, think about the mix of personalities; you want everyone to get along. Before they have said yes, be clear about what you want them to do – and be realistic about how much of their time and effort is involved.

Bridesmaids, whatever their age, are traditionally expected to pay for their dress and all their accessories. So bear this in mind when shopping; it's not very fair to demand that they wear your idea of the perfect dress if it is going to cost them a lot of money. You may need to offer to help out financially if you don't want to compromise your style ideas.

If you want only one bridesmaid or perhaps none at all, you risk offending some of your close family and friends. Handle the situation carefully, calling anyone you know is waiting to be asked to explain the situation. The size or formality of the day may mean lots of maids just won't work. Or you can explain that you are just having your sister as chief bridesmaid but, of course, their input is invaluable. Perhaps they could give a reading or sing a solo at the ceremony. Hopefully they will understand and still come along as an honoured guest.

The bridesmaids' role

Their specific wedding duties include the following:

- Offering to help with any tasks that need doing, from making favours to helping put up fairy lights at the reception venue.
- Helping the chief bridesmaid to organise the hen night.
- Shopping with the bride and chief bridesmaid for suitable bridesmaids' dresses and accessories.
- Thinking about appropriate make-up and a suitable hairstyle (you are going to have to live with the photographs for many years to come).
- Helping the bride and any younger maids get ready on the wedding morning.
- Leaving for the ceremony with the bride's mother and other bridesmaids.
- Walking down the aisle in front of or behind the bride.
- At the reception, making sure everyone has someone to talk to and looks happy and comfortable.
- Keeping an eye on younger bridesmaids and offering to help keep them amused, if necessary.
- Keeping the dancing going if the dance floor empties at any point.

The ushers

Ushers tend only to be part of a church wedding, though they can have a role to play at a larger civil ceremony. They are usually brothers and friends of the bride and groom and they take their lead on what to wear from the groom and the best man. Traditional attire for the ushers is formal wear (usually hired at the same time as the rest of the bridal party) with accessories in the wedding colour scheme.

The ushers' main duty is to arrive at the ceremony venue half an hour before the wedding to welcome guests and to show them where to sit; it is a nice touch if an usher escorts any unaccompanied female guests right to her place. Traditionally the bride's family and friends to sit on the left side of the room and the groom's family and friends on the right. Ushers should hand an order of service to each guest as he or she arrives. If the ceremony is taking place at a different place to the reception, ushers liaise with the best man to ensure all the guests have transport.

At the reception, the ushers are seated with the bridesmaids and it's their job to mingle with the other guests and make sure everyone is having a good time.

Flower girls and the ring bearer

Involving small children in your wedding guarantees some great photographs and some definite 'ahh' moments throughout the day. Just remember that little ones, however cute, are unpredictable and won't necessarily follow your carefully planned timetable of events.

All tasks need to be age-appropriate; the under-fours for example, are too small to be expected to perform.

Flower girls are usually between five and ten years old and walk down the aisle just before the bride scattering flower petals from a basket for the bride to walk on. You can have just one, but it usually works better with two or even three flower girls to give each other moral support. The flower girls' parents should be seated near the front of the proceedings so they can wave encouragement. The girls then sit with their parents for the ceremony.

> **_Real Bride's Hot Tip_**
> 66 _Being a bridesmaid is expensive – the dress, the shoes, the hen weekend. I told mine that their support was more than enough and a wedding present was definitely not expected._99
> **Gabby Mason, Manchester**

The ring bearer is usually a little boy aged between four and seven (try asking anyone older and he's likely to laugh at you!). His role is to walk down the aisle with, or just behind, the flower girls, bearing the wedding rings on an ornate cushion. Many couples actually use fake rings, preferring the moment to be symbolic rather than trusting their expensive bands to the care of a small child.

The parents

At the traditional wedding, the bride's father pretty much paid for everything and the bride's mother made most the arrangements. How times have changed! How much or how little your parents are involved in the run-up to the wedding is up to you. Just remember, the more they contribute financially, the more they are likely to want to be involved in decision-making so, if the thought of your mother on the phone 'advising' you every minute of the day fills you with horror, think twice about accepting that large contribution.

Mother of the bride

Your mother can be your greatest ally as you plan your wedding, providing you get on and she has lots of time to help. She will be there as you make key decisions about everything from your dress to the flowers. Listen to her opinion and give everything she tells you careful consideration. Experience counts for a lot so don't be too quick to dismiss her ideas.

Decide together on what type of role you want your mother to have and the tasks you want to make her responsibility. This can include any or all of the following:

- Contributing to the wedding budget.
- Looking for potential wedding suppliers – everything from the venue to the florist and catering company.
- Compiling the family section of the guest list. Helping with trimming the guest list and, if necessary, talking to the groom's family about number limitations.
- Being a shoulder for her daughter to cry on when it all gets too much.
- Shopping for the wedding dress and accessories.
- Shopping for her own outfit.
- Helping to address and post the invitations.
- Keeping track of the invitation RSVP list and managing the gift list.
- Travelling to the ceremony with the bridesmaids.
- Walking her daughter down the aisle if the bride's father is absent (both parents walk the bride down the aisle at a Jewish wedding).
- Sitting in the pew directly in front of the ceremony. Walking out first after the bride and groom once the ceremony is over.
- Standing in the receiving line, if there is one.
- Sitting at the top table during the meal.
- Dancing with the groom's father and the groom as the dancing begins.
- Making sure all gifts received from guests at the reception are taken home and stored safely.
- Reminding her daughter – at least ten times during the day – how beautiful, wonderful and special she is.

Father of the bride

As well as signing the cheques, your father's traditional role would have been to give you away at the ceremony and make a speech at the reception. And for many dads this is pretty much all the involvement he will want.

However, if he wants to play a bigger role in your day, there's no reason why he shouldn't do many of the same tasks as your mother, such as:

- Contributing to the wedding budget.
- Helping to find potential resources, particularly the venue, the entertainment and the caterers.
- Helping to compile the family section of the guest list. Helping with trimming the guest list and, if necessary, talking to the groom's family about number limitations.
- Finding the perfect outfit, including arranging suit hire if necessary.
- Accompanying his daughter to the ceremony.
- Walking his daughter down the aisle and giving her away to the groom (both parents walk the bride down the aisle at a Jewish wedding).
- Sitting in the pew immediately in front of the ceremony. Walking out first behind the bride and groom once the ceremony is over.
- Standing in the receiving line, if there is one.
- Sitting at the top table during the meal.
- Giving a simple speech, thanking everyone for coming, proposing a toast and then introducing the groom to say a few words.
- Dancing with the groom's mother and the bride as the evening begins.
- Helping to ensure all gifts received at the reception are transported home and stored safely.
- Staying until the very end of the evening, ensuring everything is paid for and, if clearing up is part of the deal, that this has been done.

A question of belonging

Do you want your father to give you away? It's a notion that fills some girls with joy – and strikes others as terribly old fashioned and even slightly insulting. You can walk down with aisle with one or two parents, your bridesmaid, your groom or alone. It is totally up to you.

The mother and father of the groom

The groom's parents traditionally don't have a big part to play in their son's wedding but these days, with them perhaps contributing an equal share of the wedding budget, there's no reason why they shouldn't be just as involved as the bride's parents. The only duties that it would usually be inappropriate for the father of the groom to perform would be giving the bride away and making a speech at the reception.

Other leading roles

There aren't enough major roles for everyone, even at a big wedding, and one way to involve valued family and friends who aren't necessarily suited to being a bridesmaid or best man is to ask them to give a reading at the ceremony. Short poems and meaningful readings are an important part of any wedding day, whether civil or religious, and can make all the difference to the tone and mood of your celebrations.

> ### Real Bride's Hot Tip
> ❝I had a huge row with my mum a month before the wedding. Looking back I realise it was silly but I was feeling so stressed about everything, she was easy to shout at. Luckily we both got over it and we can laugh about it now.❞
>
> Carly Logan, Glasgow

Anyone undertaking a reading needs to be a confident speaker with a loud, clear voice. Get them involved in what they will read – they may even come up with some good suggestions of their own. Ask them to practise their reading several times beforehand, preferably in front of other people who will be able to gauge if they are speaking at the right speed and whether their voice can easily be heard across a church, synagogue or a large room. The more they gain confidence, the better their performance will be on the day.

If you have a particularly talented musical friend then asking him or her to perform at the wedding is another lovely way to make the day feel very personal. Singing a few verses of an appropriate song or playing a musical instrument is a nice touch and one that will long be remembered by you and your guests. Just be sure the person you ask is up to the task. Performing in your living room is one thing: singing at the front of a church full of people is quite another!

Family fallings-out

Getting married is stressful for everyone involved and there are bound to be times when you feel like running away and forgetting the whole thing. But don't worry; this is quite normal. In fact, if you don't feel like throttling someone somewhere along the line you would be very unusual!

Whatever is causing the problem, don't let it drag on. A small problem may become a big problem if you let it fester. Face up to it as soon as possible and talk it through with anyone involved.

If you know it's going to be a difficult conversation, invite along a level-headed 'third party' such as your mum or your best friend who may be able to offer a more objective, less heated viewpoint. Work out what you want to say beforehand and then be prepared to listen; you may not be right!

When the problem is between you and your fiancé, the answer is often to put some distance between the two of you and the wedding. Take yourselves off for a night and agree not to talk about the wedding the whole time you are away. Hopefully, time alone together will remind you of why you wanted to get married in the first place and the whole issue of what to serve as the main course and whether or not to have a pay bar will start to seem less important.

*Michelle Head &
Stephen Brownrigg*

*Wiston House,
West Sussex*

Chapter 5

Your Ceremony

Your stress levels (and bank balance) may make you forget that the ceremony is actually the most important part of your wedding day. That magical moment when you take your vows and become man and wife is what getting married is all about.

You have three choices of ceremony venue when it comes to getting married in England, Wales and Northern Ireland: a religious ceremony in a church, synagogue or chapel; a civil wedding in a licensed building; or a civil ceremony in a register office. Weddings held in Scotland are governed by a different set of laws which are explained below.

Sit down with your partner and talk through which type of ceremony might be right for you. If you still cannot decide or have any doubts about your options, make appointments with your local registrar and your local minister. They will be able to provide some expert guidance and advice.

In England, Wales and Northern Ireland you can't get married outdoors, for example on the beach or in a garden where no specific address for the ceremony can be given. In Scotland you can get married wherever you like and you can have either a religious or a civil ceremony in the place of your choosing, including outside in the open, as long as the officiant is legally recognised and there are two witnesses present. There is talk of relaxing the marriage laws in England, Wales and Northern Ireland but at the time of writing there is no date for this to be implemented.

Religious ceremonies – the basics

Whether you have a religious or a civil ceremony is entirely a matter for you and your partner to decide, though of course the decision is likely to be more straightforward if you have religious convictions. Try not to feel pressurised by your family into agreeing to a religious service if it doesn't feel right. Explain your reasons and ask that they respect your decision; it is your wedding, after all.

A Church of England ceremony

As long as one of you lives in the parish and is on the electoral roll, you should be able to marry in your local church. You don't have to attend church regularly, though some ministers may insist on it so do check first. The banns – the public announcement of your intention to marry – will be read out in the church on three consecutive Sundays, following which the marriage must take place within three months. It's usual for you both to attend church on at least one of these occasions to hear your banns being read. If one of you lives in a different parish the

Marriage legalities

To be legally married in the UK you need to comply with the following rules:

- You and your fiancé must be at least 16 years old (in England, Wales and Northern Ireland, if either of you is under 18, a parent or guardian must give their consent).
- You must not be closely related.
- In England, Wales and Northern Ireland the marriage must take place in premises where the ceremony can legally be solemnised (register offices, premises licensed for marriage, parish churches and other places of worship registered for marriage). In Scotland you can marry anywhere providing there is a minister and witnesses present.
- The ceremony must take place in the presence of a registrar or authorised person such as a priest or rabbi.
- In England, Wales and Northern Ireland the ceremony must take place between 8am and 6pm. In Scotland there are no time restrictions.
- Two witnesses must be present.
- You must both be free and eligible to marry.

banns must be read there too, though not necessarily on the same Sundays.

If the church you want to marry in is outside the parish in which you live and you are not on the electoral register, you will need to apply for a special licence from the Archbishop of Canterbury showing a long-standing connection with the preferred church. It just being close to your reception venue will not be deemed a good enough reason!

If either of you is divorced and your former partner is still alive you will find it difficult to have a full marriage service in a Church of England church. Some ministers may make exceptions but it will always be judged on a case-by-case basis. The most likely scenario is to have a small register office ceremony first followed by a church blessing.

At the time of going to press, the costs for a Church of England wedding are £18 for the publication of the banns and a further £12 for a certificate of banns.

The marriage service costs £218 and the marriage certificate is £7. If you want bell ringers, charges vary but expect to pay about £100. A choir costs anything from £50 to £150 and a soloist much the same again. You may also incur a small location hire fee, a charge for an organist and, in winter, a small charge for additional heating.

A Roman Catholic wedding

The requirements for a Roman Catholic wedding are much the same as those for a Church of England wedding. Arrange to meet your priest as soon as you can once you are engaged, taking with you both your baptism and confirmation certificates. Most priests are empowered to act as registrars so the civil aspect of the wedding is also covered.

If you are both Roman Catholic the ceremony is usually part of a Nuptial Mass where you both receive communion, though you can be married without a full Mass if you prefer. If one of you isn't Catholic, you'll need a dispensation from the priest for a 'mixed marriage', which is usually performed outside of the Mass in a ceremony that involves no communion.

The ceremony – useful contacts

Baptists' Union	01235 517700	
British Humanist Association	020 7079 3580	www.humanism.org.uk
Church of England	020 7898 1000	www.cofe.anglican.org
Church of Scotland	01312 255722	
General Register Office (GRO) for England and Wales	01514 714200	www.ons.gov.uk
GRO for Guernsey	01481 725277	
GRO for Jersey	01534 502335	
GRO for Northern Ireland	02890 252000	
GRO for Scotland	01313 144447	
Greek Archdiocese	020 7723 4787	www.nostos.com/church
Jewish Marriage Council	020 8203 6311	www.somethingjewish.co.uk
Methodist Church	020 7222 8010	
United Reform Church	020 7916 2020	

The Roman Catholic Church has strict rules about divorce and does not allow the remarriage of divorcees. Exceptions are occasionally made if your first marriage was not recognised by the Church, but you should consult your priest for advice.

Other religions

For all religious weddings other than Church of England or Roman Catholic, the legal requirements are the same for civil ceremonies and you need to apply to the religious authority at your place of worship as well as the local superintendent registrar. To find out more and for information on inter-faith marriages, see the useful contacts box opposite for who can help you.

Civil ceremonies – the basics

Over half of all weddings in the UK are currently non-religious. If you don't want to have a religious ceremony or are prevented from doing so because of divorce or mixed faith, then the alternative is a civil wedding. This takes the form of a register office ceremony or a ceremony performed in a building that holds a marriage licence. In either case, the procedure for arranging everything is the same.

> ### *Real Bride's Hot Tip*
> *❝Ask your registrar for advice on any aspect of the wedding ceremony. They are very helpful and can save you hours of worry.❞*
>
> *Sharon Newman,*
> *Harrogate, Yorkshire*

Your first step is to contact the superintendent registrar for your district, which you must have lived in for a minimum of seven days. Even if both of you live in the same district, each of you needs your own superintendent registrar's certificate so both bride and groom must apply in person to the local office. Couples then wait 15 days for the certificates to be issued – this is known as the notice period – and your notices of marriage are displayed on a notice board in the register office during this period. You can hold the marriage ceremony any time after the 15-day notice period is over and the notice is valid for 12 months.

At this first appointment you can also check that your preferred date is free, available times and that a registrar is able to attend your venue if you want to have a wedding in a licensed building. This last point is very important and you should never book your venue until you know that the registrar is able to marry you on a

particular date. If you are marrying out of your district you'll need to speak to the superintendent registrar in that area about booking a ceremony.

If you haven't yet decided on a venue, the registrar will be able to give you a list of licensed premises within your district. For a full list of over 3,000 countrywide premises licensed for marriage visit www.gro.gov.uk/gro/content/marriages, which tells you how to obtain the list for a small fee.

At the time of going to press, the costs for a civil ceremony are £30 per person to give notice of your marriage, and a register office fee ranging from about £40 on a weekday up to about £250 at weekends. Civil ceremonies at a licensed venue are more expensive and cost up to £400 at weekends, though prices vary considerably around the country. You also have to pay £7 for the marriage certificate at either type of ceremony.

In special circumstances such as serious illness, you can apply for a registrar's general licence, which allows a marriage to take place anywhere at any time and this is usually valid for 12 months.

The religious wedding ceremony

The traditional religious ceremony follows much the same format as it has done for many years, with the addition of readings and hymns to make it personal to you. Chat through your options with the minister and get his or her agreement for everything you want to include. If you feel uncomfortable with a particular phrase, ask about making a change. Most brides prefer to say 'love, honour and cherish' rather than 'obey', for instance, and it is usual for you both to promise to bestow all your worldly goods. In times gone by, only the groom offered this!

It is usual to give your guests an order of service sheet on arrival so they can follow proceedings and it's a good idea to include the words of hymns, unless you want a lot of mumbling when not everyone knows the words. The names of the officiant, anyone giving the readings and the organist are usually included as well. Your minister will be able to tell you if you need copyright clearance to reproduce the hymns on your order of service – a small fee is payable to the copyright holder for the use of any words for the 70 years following the death of the writer. However, this doesn't apply if you just want to sing the hymns or use a hymn book.

Music for a religious ceremony is usually supplied by an organist, a choir or perhaps a string quartet. If you want something more contemporary to accompany you down the aisle, most churches have the facility for playing CDs but do check first that your musical choices are acceptable to your minister.

Order of service

The traditional order of service follows this format:

Processional (entrance of the bride)
Introduction
Hymn (with the words)
The Marriage
Prayers
Reading (optional)
Blessing (optional)
Hymn (with the words)
Reading or blessing (optional)
Signing of the register
Recessional (exit of the bride and groom)

Your Ceremony

Musical suggestions

All these pieces of music are suitable for a religious ceremony, and many also suit a civil ceremony but do check with your registrar first.

The prelude (arrival of the guests)

Jesu, Joy of Man's Desiring – Bach
Sheep May Safely Graze – Bach
Wachet Auf – Bach
Cantilène Nuptial – Dubois
Chanson de Matin – Elgar
Nimrod from the Enigma Variations – Elgar
Pavane – Fauré
Ave Maria – Gounod
Largo – Handel
Water Music – Handel
Ave Verum Corpus – Mozart
Voce Sapete – Mozart
Canon in D – Pachelbel
The Swan – Saint Saens
Ave Maria – Schubert
Greensleeves – Vaughan Williams

The processional (walking up the aisle)

Trumpet Tune – Charpentier
Trumpet Voluntary (Prince of Denmark's March) – Clarke
Morning from Peer Gynt – Grieg
Arrival of the Queen of Sheba – Handel
Trumpet Minuet – Hollins
I Was Glad – Parry
Trumpet Tune – Purcell
Trumpet Voluntary – Stanley
Spring from the Four Seasons – Vivaldi
Winter from the Four Seasons – Vivaldi
Wedding March from Lohengrin (Here Comes The Bride) – Wagner

Your Ceremony

The signing of the register

Any of the pieces suitable for the Prelude would also be ideal for the time when the wedding party is in the registry. Others are:

Air on the G String – Bach
Claire de Lune – Debussy
Flower Duet from Lakmé – Delibes
Panis Angelicus – Franck
Air from the Water Music – Handel
Exsultate Jubilate – Mozart
The Lord Bless You and Keep You – Rutter

The recessional (as you leave as man and wife)

Ode to Joy – Beethoven
Pomp and Circumstance March No 4 – Elgar
March from Scipio – Handel
The Rejoicing Music from the Royal Fireworks – Handel
Bridal March – Hollins
Wedding March from A Midsummer Night's Dream – Mendelssohn
Grand March from Le Prophete – Meyerbeer
Rondeau – Mouret
Maestoso from Symphony No 3 in C – Saint Saens
Grand March from Aida – Verdi
Carillion de Westminster – Vierne
Finale from Symphony No 1 – Widor
Toccata from Symphony No 5 in F – Widor
Fanfare – Whitlock

**For more ideas and to share yours
with other brides, log on to
www.youandyourwedding.co.uk**

The civil wedding ceremony

In a civil ceremony you have more scope to personalise proceedings, even going as far as writing your own vows if you want to. Just remember this is still a legal ceremony and anything you want to include should reflect the solemnity of the occasion. Keep anything too personal or flippant for a private moment between the two of you.

Legally, a civil wedding cannot have vows, songs, poems or readings that include any religious references – and this can even include words like angel in some cases – so it's very important that you check everything you want to include with your registrar before the wedding. You generally won't be able to include anything that extends the ceremony beyond a total of about twenty minutes, sometimes even shorter if you are having a register office ceremony.

The informal nature of the civil ceremony is what attracts many couples but you should think about including a few readings or poems, otherwise the whole thing could be over so quickly that your guests will hardly have taken their seats before you have said your vows and it's time to leave for the reception.

If you are marrying in a licensed premises, the order of service can follow pretty much the same format as for a religious ceremony; it's just the words that are different and, of course, there are no hymns or prayers. A register office ceremony is usually much simpler but most locations will have a CD player so you can choose some favourite music to play as you come in and leave.

A humanist ceremony

If you want complete freedom about what you say to one another – and where you say it – you could think about having a humanist ceremony. This can be

performed anywhere, including outdoors, though your vows would not be legally recognised so you would need to have a civil ceremony, usually in a register office, beforehand. Contact the British Humanist Association (www.humanism.org.uk) for more details about what is involved and how to arrange a celebrant to conduct the ceremony.

A wedding abroad

If neither type of traditional ceremony appeals to you and you fancy something different, tying the knot abroad is an increasingly popular choice for many UK couples. It is estimated that around 30,000 couples are currently choosing this option and it is particularly popular for second marriages and for older couples who don't want the fuss and organisation of a traditional wedding. The world is your oyster, with locations as diverse as the Empire State Building in New York to a remote palm-fringed beach in the Caribbean.

Most major tour operators have a weddings department, with specialists on hand to answer your questions and to make all the arrangements for you. The paperwork involved in a foreign wedding is fairly straightforward but it's a good idea to consult a professional to ensure you haven't missed anything. In most destinations it's possible to arrange a civil or religious ceremony and, as long as the marriage is legally recognised in the country in which it takes place, it's deemed valid in the UK as well. If you have any queries, check with your local register office or contact the tourist board of the country you intend to visit for details.

Real Bride's Hot Tip
“Check beforehand if anyone else is marrying on the same day as you. We were a bit disappointed to find we were one of three weddings in one afternoon. Everything did feel a little rushed.”
Denise Morrison, Cardiff

In recent years, Europe has become the hot favourite for many couples planning a wedding abroad. With the advent of cheaper flights and a relaxation in the European marriage law a few years ago, it is possible to have a weekend wedding

Top wedding hot spots abroad

Australia	Malta
The Caribbean	Mauritius
Cyprus	Sri Lanka
Greece	Thailand
Italy	USA

accompanied by a large group of guests for much the same budget as for a UK wedding – with sunshine virtually guaranteed!

If you are planning a wedding abroad, do your homework first in exactly the same way as you would for a wedding at home. Most of the major resorts offer a wedding package, often combined with a honeymoon, so find out exactly what is included in the price and what will cost extra. The basic package usually includes all paperwork, the ceremony, a bouquet, a buttonhole for the groom, sparkling wine for a toast, a wedding cake and a photographer who will take a set number of shots. Most resorts offer a civil ceremony at the hotel but can also arrange a religious ceremony or a blessing in a local church if you prefer.

Ask whether there's an on-site wedding co-ordinator to help you once you are there and, if you have your heart set on a particular detail, make sure you ask whether it will be possible before you finalise any arrangements. Most resorts offer a number of different locations where you can hold the ceremony, which you'll be shown on arrival.

If you are marrying in a hot country, make sure you both choose outfits that suit the temperature. Brides should look for dresses in cool, uncrushable fabrics like silk or chiffon, wear minimal make-up and choose a simple, unfussy hairstyle. The groom should think about ditching a jacket and wearing lighter colours than the traditional black or navy blue. Linen trousers, a white shirt, perhaps a waistcoat and loafers is a stylish option that will guarantee he feels cool and looks good.

If you arrive at your wedding destination with a day or two to spare, be sensible and don't spent all the time in the sun; bright red faces and tan lines won't look good in your photographs!

Charlotte Homan
& Carl Richardson

Gorse Lodge,
Lincolnshire

Chapter 6

Your Suppliers

This section is all about putting together your dream wedding team – the individuals and companies you pay to help turn your dreams into reality. Choose the right people and their expertise will ease your stress and in many cases save you money too.

Your vision of a perfect day will remain just that unless you assemble a team of experts around you to help turn that dream into reality. You only have to hear one bride crying about her fuzzy photographs or disappointing food to realise that you can't trust your day to just anyone. Experienced professionals are essential to any wedding; they will guide you as you form your ideas, add their own expertise and, most importantly, make it all happen on the wedding day.

After you have decided on the basics such as the style, size, time and venue for your ceremony and reception, you need to find a team of people you can trust to listen to you beforehand, work with you during the planning stages, and then come through with flying colours on the day.

So where do you find your dream team? Word-of-mouth recommendation from recently married friends is invaluable, and ask your venue for its recommendations too. Many will have a list of preferred suppliers with whom they have worked in the past. You don't have to use them – but a team of people who have worked together before could make your life much easier. Once you have made a list of potential companies, ask them for references and call some of their previous clients to ask what they thought of the service they received.

Did the supplier do everything promised at the outset? Was everything done on time and on budget? What was the best thing about them? What was the worst thing? Would they book them again?

Before deciding on anyone, get a couple of estimates so you can compare prices and services. You may be surprised at the difference in what is and isn't included – and the cheapest price may not be your best option. Bear in mind that a higher price often means the supplier is taking on more responsibility, freeing up your time and energy for other things.

The first meeting

You and your fiancé should meet all potential major suppliers together. Arrange a time for when neither of you is in a rush and be clear on what you want. That means knowing the proposed wedding date, a rough idea of overall style, the number of guests and, of course, how much you have to spend.

Your budget is a very important part of these initial discussions and you have to be honest. A good supplier will have creative ideas about how to get the most for your money. If you feel someone is pressurising you to spend more, save yourselves time and hassle and look elsewhere. Ask for photographs or recordings of previous weddings, and samples to see, hear or taste.

This first meeting is a good time to assess whether you get on with the person sitting in front of you. You will be spending a lot of time together so you need to know that your personalities and sense of style are compatible. This is why it's so important that you meet whoever will be your main contact at this initial meeting. Some photographic studios can be a bit vague about which photographer will actually be at your wedding; this is not good enough. The venue may say it has more than one event co-ordinator, in which case you need to know which one and get some assurance that the person you have met, and liked, will be available.

The fine print

When it comes to a wedding there's no room for error and the right paperwork goes a long way in helping to ensure the professionals you have chosen come through on the day. Every couple needs to be clear about what they want and to confirm everything in writing. Read everything carefully and don't sign until you are completely satisfied it is a reflection of all you have discussed at your initial meetings. Be sure all the basic details are included such as names, addresses, dates, venues, services to be provided, timings, costs (including VAT), and agreed extras. Make sure you keep a copy of all receipts and correspondence as proof of arrangements agreed and any payments made for deposits.

Finally, take out some form of wedding insurance. You wouldn't dream of buying a car without insurance, yet many couples are happy to risk anything up to £20,000 when it comes to their wedding. The average policy covers most eventualities and for under £100 it is well worth the investment.

Your Suppliers

Your venue

Everything to do with the venue is covered more fully in Chapter 3, Your Venue, page 38, but, in the context of this section, here are some tips on the people you will be dealing with at the venue, rather than the location itself.

Your main contacts at any venue will be the manager and the on-site events co-ordinator, if there is one. These are the people who will show you around the venue at your first meeting and answer everything about facilities and prices. Arm yourself with a list of what you need to know and gauge how well the people answer your questions. Are they self-assured and knowledgeable about the organisation? Do they seem flexible and willing to accommodate any more unusual suggestions such as a firework party or putting up a marquee? If things are not possible for a good reason that's fine: but if they act as if everything seems just too much trouble that's quite another matter and should set your alarm bells ringing.

Ask who will be your main contact as the plans progress and whether they will be assigned to your wedding all the way through. You need the reassurance that the person who has been involved in your plans will be around to ensure the smooth running of the day from the minute your guests arrive to when they leave.

Your wedding photographer

The photographs of your wedding will become one of your most treasured possessions and brides who scrimp on this are nearly always disappointed. Yes, it is expensive – but you can't go back and do it all again if the photographs are too dark or are out of focus. Trust a professional rather than a talented friend; you get what you pay for and this is one area of your wedding where you shouldn't compromise if at all possible.

You may think the photographer is pretty low on your 'to do' list but popular wedding photographers get booked up quickly so it is important to start looking as soon as possible. Decide on the style of pictures you prefer. Do you want traditional shots or a more relaxed, reportage style? Do you want everything in colour or a mixture of black and white and colour? Choose someone who specialises in your preferred look. Reportage photography may look easy but it takes a certain skill to capture 'unposed' moments well.

❝ *Your wedding album will become one
of your most treasured possessions.* **❞**

One thing that takes a lot of couples by surprise with their photography is that they don't own the copyright after the wedding, which means you don't get the negatives or images on disk and you have to pay for each print made. This should all be made clear in the initial agreement, including the number of prints included in the package price.

Styles of wedding photography

Old-school romantic Not every bride wants contemporary pictures. There's a lot to be said for traditional and shamelessly romantic shots, so long as they are not clichéd and the quality is excellent.

Reportage This candid style of photography is very popular. Photographers who specialise in this look are intent on capturing the impromptu moments to create a storybook feel of the wedding. From the bride getting ready with her maids to the best man sneakily practising his speech behind the marquee, you will end up with a true flavour of the whole day.

Black and white Even if you love colour prints and want the world to see how much effort you have put into colour co-ordinating everything to perfection, it's still a good idea to include a few black and white shots as well. With the ability to throw atmospheric contrasts of light and dark, the overall effect can be very stylish and flattering.

Sepia These are instantly recognisable brownish or blueish shots, reminiscent of very early photographic styles. White dresses appear ivory and the soft tones are usually very flattering.

Hand tinting This is a special technique applied to black and white prints where the photographer adds splashes of colour; for example, only the bouquet is in colour on a black and white shot.

Digital images Many photographers these days will use a digital camera. Computer techniques allow for the removal of blemishes and 'red eye', the bride and groom can be superimposed on to a different location, and the sky turned an amazing shade of blue – whatever your heart desires.

Must-have wedding photographs

It's a good idea to put together a list of pictures you really want taken during the course of the day. Give a copy of your list to the photographer and give another copy to the best man who can make sure all the key members of the bridal party have been included on several occasions.

Suggested photographs include:

- the bride and bridesmaids getting ready
- the wedding dress and accessories
- the bridal bouquet
- the bride's mother and the bridesmaids leaving for the ceremony
- the bride and her father leaving for the ceremony
- the groom and best man getting ready
- the groom and best man outside the ceremony
- the wedding rings on a cushion or prayer book
- the wedding transport
- the bride arriving at the ceremony
- the bride walking down the aisle
- the ceremony
- signing the register
- the first married kiss
- the bride and groom and their families outside the ceremony
- the couple and the main bridal party
- the bride and her parents
- the groom and his parents
- the couple and both sets of parents

- the couple and respective work colleagues
- the couple with all their guests (if room allows)
- the reception venue before the guests arrive
- close-up details of the tables, favours, menu cards etc.
- the wedding cake
- the entrance of the bride and groom to the reception
- the top table
- the speeches
- the toast
- the couple cutting the cake
- the first dance as man and wife
- the couple leaving at the end of the reception

The videographer

If you are having a wedding video, you may well choose a videographer who works at the same studio as the photographer. Or your photographer can probably recommend someone he or she has worked with in the past. It's important that the two of them have a good working rapport since you don't want them getting in each other's way.

Ask to see samples of the videographer's work. As with the photographer, you want to see a complete example of their work – a whole video, not carefully edited highlights from several weddings. You'll be paying as much for the post-production (that is, the work done back in the studio after the wedding) as for the footage that is shot on the day. The addition of background music, special effects such as slow motion and captions can make your video look more like a feature film than a home movie.

Real Bride's Hot Tip

❝ We didn't think we wanted a video but it was money well spent. All our guests were asked to say something on camera and their good wishes have made a fantastic memento. ❞

John and Amanda Douglas, Portsmouth

The florist

Flowers play an essential part in any wedding and the key to the best wedding flowers is finding the right florist, someone who shares your vision and has lots of ideas. Start your search six to nine months before the wedding and expect to finalise all the main details about three weeks before the big day.

Make a clippings book of bouquets and arrangements you like – and those you don't – to give potential florists an idea of the style you are looking for. At your first meeting it's also a good idea to take along a picture of your dress, details of the venues and swatches of fabric for colour matching.

Most florists will have a portfolio of previous work (be suspicious if they don't), which will give you a good indication of their type of work. Describe the look you want and be honest about what you want to spend. Any good florist should be able to come up with plenty of ideas for the bouquet and centrepieces that work within your budget and suit your favoured colour scheme. Once booked, the florist should be happy to mock up the bridal bouquet and one of the centrepieces so you can see exactly what they are proposing.

If your florist hasn't worked at your venues before, be sure they can visit them with you before the wedding. Find out how much time your florist will have to set up and decorate each room and how much help he or she will need to get it all done in plenty of time.

Once you have accepted your florist's ideas and the price, get confirmation of all the details in writing. You will want specific flowers to be detailed and what alternatives may have to be used in the event that something isn't available – you definitely don't want to find your white roses being substituted for white carnations without prior discussion! Most florists – although not all – will expect a 20 per cent deposit at the time of accepting the quotation, with the balance payable two or three weeks before the wedding. Double check the small print about the cancellation policy.

The caterers

The caterers are an essential part of your wedding team. The food you serve your guests can make or break your reception and it is likely to account for the largest slice of your wedding budget, so what they do has to be excellent.

You are likely to be choosing from two different types of caterer: the in-house caterer based at the venue; and the off-site catering company which brings everything to your venue.

Many venues offer wedding packages, ranging in price depending on the style and formality of the event and the ingredients being used. Generally speaking, the more formal the occasion, the more the catering is going to cost you. Most packages include all the food, the people to cook and serve it, the tables, chairs, linens, china, cutlery, glasses and bar staff – all priced on a 'per head' basis. But, if you want to use items outside the usual package, such as coloured linens, specific glasses or having chair covers, you can list everything you want and have it priced individually.

Depending on the venue, you may not have to use its in-house catering facilities. But if you particularly want to bring in someone of your own, you are likely to be charged a lot for the privilege and it may be more cost-effective and a lot less hassle to look for a different venue.

If you are holding the reception in an unfurnished venue, such as a marquee at home or the village hall, you will probably use a mixture of hire companies and outside caterers. The room will be a blank space so you'll need to hire everything from the tables and chairs to the linens and glasses. Some catering companies can help with all of this, others just provide food. This style of reception obviously

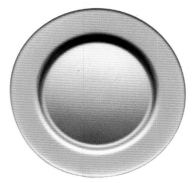

involves more organisation and, unless you have lots of time, you may find hiring a wedding organiser worthwhile. What they save you in stress and time could well be worth their fee.

Once you have a shortlist of caterers or venues, ask for a tasting session of the proposed menu and drink options. Discuss the menu, canapés, guest

numbers, vegetarian and special dietary options and when you need to confirm final numbers. Don't be afraid to make changes to their food suggestions; it's your wedding and you need to love, not just like, what you are serving your friends and family. They are professionals and won't be offended if you want something different on the menu.

As with all your suppliers, ask for a full quotation in writing including everything that has been discussed at your various meetings. Expect to pay anything up to 50 per cent when you book, with the balance due when you confirm the final guest numbers about two weeks before the wedding. Check all the small print for things like overtime rates and details of the cancellation policy.

Wedding transport

You will probably want to arrive at the wedding in style so you need to invest in some form of wedding transport. An elegant car is the most usual option and most car hire companies have a suitable Mercedes, Audi or Rolls Royce that can be dressed with ribbon for the occasion. There are also lots of special car hire companies providing vintage cars that could bring a lovely romantic touch to the day. Just make sure any car you are using can accommodate your dress without crushing the fabric too much; you don't want to arrive in a crumpled mess!

When you book a car, ask whether the company charges by the hour or per job so you can work out how much it will cost to be collected from home and taken to the venue and on to the reception. It is usual to provide a car for the mother of the bride and the bridesmaids as well, in which case you may be offered a better rate for booking two vehicles.

Your groom might like to splash out and hire himself a sports car to take him and his best man to the ceremony. It's a pricey idea but he'll love having the chance to drive a Ferrari or an E-Type Jaguar for the day – and, of course, you get to travel in it too if you are leaving the reception to go off to your first night hotel.

Other popular forms of wedding transport include a horse and carriage, a stretch limousine or a white London taxi. Hiring a red Routemaster bus to ferry your guests from the church to the reception venue is a nice idea and again looks great in your photographs.

A hot air balloon and a helicopter are two more dramatic forms of transport but do make sure you check with the venue beforehand that the grounds are suitable. And remember: balloons can't fly in certain weather conditions so you may need an alternative up your sleeve on a bad day.

Musicians and entertainers

Music is the soundtrack to your wedding day so you'll want it to be just right. Think about the key moments during your day when music will be appropriate: as you walk down the aisle; during the ceremony and to entertain your guests while you are signing the register; at the reception during cocktails; during the meal; then, of course, to entertain your guests through the evening. Don't feel you have to have live music throughout the day; this would be expensive and really isn't necessary.

Recommendations from relatives and friends can help you find the best entertainers but, once you have narrowed down a shortlist, it's important that you hear them play, live if possible, and don't rely on someone else's opinion. You are looking for music that will suit the tastes of all your guests so a middle-of-the-road route is usually your safest option. It may not be the hippest entertainment your younger friends will have experienced but there's nothing worse than an empty dance floor or your older relatives all wanting to leave early because they are being deafened by a rock band.

Before booking anyone for the ceremony and the reception, check with the officiant and the venue about any restrictions on numbers and noise levels. Let potential performers know how many guests are coming and where and for how long you want them to play.

Most standard wedding bands and DJs have a favoured play list, so make sure you look through this and delete any songs you detest.

Music isn't the only way of entertaining your guests at the reception. There are lots of magicians, mime artists and caricaturists who can walk around as your guests eat, entertaining each table. It all depends on the amount of entertainment you want to offer and, of course, your budget.

The toastmaster

A toastmaster (also known as a master of ceremonies) is a nice addition to a more formal wedding. Toastmasters are renowned for their loud voices and it is their job to announce when dinner is served, the entrance of the bride and groom, toasts and a blessing (if you want one), and to make any general announcements such as when it's time for cutting the cake.

A toastmaster will be smartly dressed in a signature red jacket, white shirt and black trousers and many couples have found having one invaluable for keeping the wedding in order and running smoothly. Find out more from the National Association of Toastmasters website (www.natuk.com).

The wedding organiser

More and more couples are turning to a professional to organise some or all of their wedding. They are experts in managing suppliers and often have great contacts, saving you money by guiding you in the right direction to suit your budget.

If you have a demanding job and want to enjoy your weekends rather than spending every waking moment meeting potential suppliers, a professional planner can be a life saver. One will also be invaluable if your wedding is being held in a different town to where you live, and absolutely essential if you are bursting with creative ideas but logistic realities elude you. A professional will help tie up all the loose ends and make sure everything runs smoothly on the day – so you can relax and enjoy your wedding.

> ### Real Bride's Hot Tip
> *We used a wedding planner because I just didn't have time and neither of us has close family who could help out. The amount of stress she saved me made it money well spent!*
>
> **Jane Pope, Whitby, Yorkshire**

The cost of a wedding planner varies but expect to pay either a set fee for a set number of tasks undertaken, or a percentage of the total budget if he or she is involved in the preparations and the wedding day.

You may need a wedding planner if:

- your wedding venue is some distance from your home or is abroad
- you have a high-pressure job and not enough time to co-ordinate everything
- you are having arguments with everyone already and you feel it would be easier to get someone else to make the decisions
- you find negotiating prices with suppliers difficult or embarrassing
- you haven't a clue where to start – on anything at all!

You don't necessarily have to commit to a wedding planner for the whole day. Some wedding organisers offer different levels of service, from just helping you source key suppliers to doing everything for you, including being there on the wedding day until the last guest leaves. Several companies offer wedding planning courses, which over a couple of days will give you the main pointers to think about as well as hints and tips on getting the best from everyone you employ.

Caroline Moore &
Jonathan Sorrell

Sevenoaks, Kent

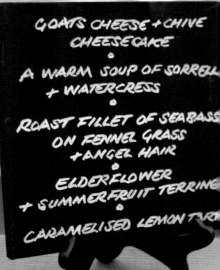

GOATS CHEESE + CHIVE
CHEESECAKE
•
A WARM SOUP OF SORRELL
+ WATERCRESS
•
ROAST FILLET OF SEABASS
ON FENNEL GRASS
+ ANGEL HAIR
•
ELDERFLOWER
+ SUMMER FRUIT TERRINE
•
CARAMELISED LEMON TART

Chapter 7

Your Reception

Your wedding reception will almost certainly be the biggest and best party of your life — not to mention the most expensive, although having a great time doesn't just revolve around spending money. There's masses to think about, so let's get you started!

The reception takes the biggest slice of the wedding budget, using around 40 per cent of your total cash, so you'll want to make sure it is money well spent. Before you make any firm plans, think about what sort of event you want. Do you see a sit-down dinner followed by disco dancing? Or is cocktails, canapés and conversation more your style?

How lavish the reception will be will depend on the size of your budget and how many guests you are inviting but it's important that it suits your personal style as well. Not everyone wants to follow tradition and party into the small hours. If you would rather have a nice lunch before leaving in the late afternoon, then that's what you should be planning. Providing you make the format of the day clear on the invitations, your guests will be happy to go along with whatever you want to do – it's your celebration, after all!

The wedding menu

So what are you going to feed your guests? The food is one of the most memorable parts of any wedding party and will long be remembered, hopefully for all the right reasons! Work with your caterers to come up with an interesting – though not too adventurous – range of dishes that will suit most tastes from young to old.

You will want to get maximum taste as well as great presentation for your money, so ask your caterers to make several suggestions, including options for your vegetarian guests. Think about the time of year; seasonal food usually works best and if it is a hot day people are more likely to want a light meal, whereas hearty fare will be most welcome on a cold winter's afternoon.

Once you have decided on your favourite menu, your caterers should offer a tasting session where you can sample the dishes and the suggested wines. Don't be afraid to say if you don't like something; they are professionals and will happily come up with an alternative.

Sit down or buffet?

The most formal style of reception will have a sit-down meal of three or four courses served by waiting staff. It's the most expensive option and is the usual choice for any meal served from mid-afternoon to early evening. A buffet is the less traditional way to offer your guests their meal. It's not necessarily a much cheaper option because you still need tables and chairs and staff to serve and then clear away the plates, but it does feel less formal and allows you to offer your guests lots of different menu choices. Food stations serving a variety of regional dishes are currently very popular: Indian, Asian, sushi, fish and chips, pizza and pasta would all go down well.

Real Bride's Hot Tip
❝ We had a buffet but with lots of waiting staff on hand to help guests carry their plates back to the tables. It was welcomed by young and old! ❞
Claire Richardson, Cardiff

If you are planning on marrying in the morning you could have a brunch-style reception serving smoked salmon, crispy bacon, scrambled eggs, bagels and eggs Benedict and set up a coffee bar to serve everyone's favourite cappuccino or latte. If you want to have an afternoon reception, which won't go on into the evening, champagne and wedding cake is one option, or offer cocktails and substantial canapés if you want to provide a little more food.

Classic menu options

You will want to work with your caterers on creating the perfect menu but these ideas may just tempt your taste buds and give you some clue as to where to start.

Your Reception

Summer menu

Whether you are having a sit-down meal or a buffet, you'll want a combination of dishes that are light yet substantial.

Starter: Parcels of crab or smoked salmon with a dill sauce, served with salad

Main course: Rack of lamb with rosemary and fresh seasonal vegetables

Dessert: Strawberries and clotted cream or ice-cream served in older-style shallow champagne glasses

Summer buffet

English glazed ham with onion marmalade and pickles

A seafood platter

Game and foie gras terrine

Quails' eggs with celery salt

Stilton with port

An assortment of salads

Grilled potatoes, flat mushrooms and a selection of interesting breads

Desserts: Gooseberry fool, white chocolate and chestnut cheesecake, bowls of fresh seasonal fruits

Delight your guests and choose menu options that look as good as they taste.

Winter menu

People tend to have larger appetites in the winter and will love it if you serve warming, comfort food.

Starter: Hot smoked salmon with avocado salsa served with potatoes

Main course: Roast duck breast with plum sauce and roasted vegetables

Dessert: Sticky toffee pudding with vanilla ice cream

Winter buffet

Potted Stilton with walnuts and oat cakes

Kippers and horseradish

Kedgeree

Game pie

Roast salmon with mustard butter

Chicken in red wine

Braised red cabbage, brussels sprouts with chestnuts and chips

Desserts: Orange and ginger pudding, chocolate torte, coffee mousse with Amaretto biscuits

Reception drinks

Alcoholic drinks are the other big part of the reception budget. You can buy your drinks direct from the venue or a catering company, or buy from the local off-licence or supermarket and take it with you. You could even take a trip to a French supermarket and buy in some alcohol (champagne, wines and beers are the best value) and there's almost no limit to the amount you can bring back as long as you make no charge for it. If you are thinking of providing your own champagne and wine be warned that most venues will charge you a corkage fee – anything up to £10 a bottle – to cover the cost of chilling, uncorking, pouring and serving it to your guests. Your cost-effective wine may not be such a bargain after all!

Champagne

Champagne is *the* wedding tipple and your guests will all want to indulge in at least one glass, even if it is just to toast the bride and groom. To be called champagne, the wine has to come from the Champagne region of France but there are lots of reasonably priced, and excellent, sparkling wines you may like to think about serving if bubbles are an important part of your celebrations.

Ask your caterer or the local off-licence for recommendations and spend a weekend or two indulging in a tasting session. Brut on the label means it's dry, demi-sec is sweet and sec is the sweetest. Pink champagne is perfect for weddings and comes in a variety of hues from the palest pastel to a deep rose. Serve well chilled in tall flutes to maximise the bubbles.

Wine and cocktails

Cocktail parties are currently very much in vogue and are a stylish way to welcome guests to the reception. Ask the bartender at your venue to come up with two or three alternatives using the classic gin, vodka and non-alcoholic mixes and then you can give each one a name, personal to you or the wedding. Who wants to drink a gin and tonic when they could be drinking a Wonderful Wedding? Just keep an eye on what the venue will be charging you for each cocktail as they tend to be easy to drink and can be pricey. If budget is a big issue, a bowl of punch – suitably named, of course – is the most cost-effective option.

> ### Real Bride's Hot Tip
> 66 We welcomed our guests with mini bottles of champagne to be drunk through a straw. Many of the older guests had never seen them before and it was a real talking point. 99
> Maureen James, London

Regardless of what food you are serving, your guests will expect to be offered a choice of red or white wine with the meal. Find out from the venue what it can offer and don't turn up your nose at the house wines; they are often good and excellent value for money. Make sure you order enough wine, allowing for about half a bottle per guest and expect to get about five glasses out of each bottle. Most venues will let you buy on a sale-or-return basis, which means you pay only for the bottles that are opened.

Soft drinks

You need to spare a thought for your guests who don't drink and for those who may be driving. In summer months in particular, everyone will welcome a glass of something non-alcoholic at some point in the evening. Water and orange juice are

the classic offerings but they are a bit dull. How about providing flavoured waters, home-made lemonade and interesting fruit cordials? You can serve them all from chilled, ice-filled jugs topped with slices of fruit.

A pay bar

One perfectly acceptable way of stretching the reception budget is to introduce a pay bar at some point in the evening. It is usual to provide your guests with a welcome drink, wine with the meal and some fizz for the toasts but once the meal is over many couples ask their guests to pay for drinks during the evening.

If the thought of a pay bar is uncomfortable, think of it like this: the reception either goes on longer and people pay for evening drinks, or have free drinks but go home early because the disco budget has been used up on booze. I'm certain most of your guests, would say they would prefer to stay and party with you!

The typical reception timetable

This will give you some idea of what happens at the traditional dinner-and-dancing type of reception, but it's up to you which parts you include.

4.00pm Arrive at the reception

The wedding party arrives at the reception followed by the guests.

4.00–4.30pm The receiving line

The bride, groom and main wedding party form a receiving line and greet guests one by one. A lot of couples choose not to have a receiving line, feeling it's too formal and time-consuming. But you can still welcome your guests with a glass of bubbly or a cocktail.

4.30–5.30pm Cocktails

The bride and groom go off with members of the main bridal party for photographs. Guests enjoy a drink and canapés and check the table plan to see where they will be sitting. A string quartet or a harpist could provide music, or you could have a sophisticated classical music CD playing in the background.

5.45pm Announcements

Dinner is announced by the toastmaster or head waiter and guests start to move into the dining area to find their seats. It is usual for both sets of parents, the best man and bridesmaids to go in first, followed by other guests. The bride and groom are announced and guests stand as they make their entrance.

6.00pm Welcome

Once the couple are seated and the room is quiet, the father of the bride or the toastmaster welcomes everyone to the wedding. A minister may say a blessing.

6.15pm Dinner is served

The first course is served to the top table, then to all the other guests. Other courses follow in good but not rushed time.

7.45pm Toasts

After dessert, glasses are refilled and the bride's father toasts the health of the bride and groom.

7.50 pm The speeches

The father of the bride makes the first speech and is followed by the groom, who responds on behalf of himself and his new wife. The groom proposes a toast to the bridesmaids and may also give out a small thank-you present to the bridesmaids, flower girls and any page boys. The best man replies on behalf of the bridesmaids and then makes his speech. If the bride wants to say a few words – and this is a growing trend – she can do this at the same time or just after her husband.

8.30 pm Cutting the cake

The bride and groom make the first cut in the wedding cake, which is then taken away by the catering staff and cut into neat pieces to serve with coffee. Any evening-only guests will usually be invited to arrive just after the cake has been cut and should be welcomed with a drink.

8.45 pm The first dance

Tables are cleared to make way for dancing. The bride and groom take the floor for their chosen first dance tune. The next dance is for the bride and her father and the groom and his mother. Other guests gradually take to the floor after the first couple of minutes.

Depending on the venue, the evening will draw to a close at a set time or may go on until dawn. If you do anticipate partying into the night remember to make it clear to your guests that you won't be leaving. It is traditional for guests to wait until after the bride and groom have left before departing themselves and older friends and those with small children will want to go home.

At an agreed time before too many guests have left, it's fun to indulge in that age-old tradition of tossing the bouquet. All the single girls crowd around the bride, who faces away from them and tosses her bouquet backwards. Tradition says whoever catches it will be the next to marry!

If you are going to leave the party before your guests, you can either slip away to change or stay in your wedding outfits to go to your first night hotel. Many couples like to make a dramatic exit and a short firework display is becoming more and more popular to signal the end of the evening.

Your wedding cake

The cake is the focal point of any reception and, whether you choose a simple tiered classic or a tower of cupcakes, you will want it to taste as good as it looks.

Think about your cake at the same time as the food menu. Your caterer may have a baker as part of the team, the venue may be able to recommend a favourite supplier, or you can find a specialist cake maker in wedding magazines and the Yellow Pages. Many high street shops also offer well-priced wedding cakes, in a variety of sizes, which can be stacked and decorated with flowers, ribbons or a mini bride and groom.

If you are using a cake maker look through his or her portfolio of work and ask to sample a selection of the cakes. Questions to ask your baker include: Do they charge per cake or per slice? What is the delivery charge? Can they provide a cake stand and knife?

An average three-tier cake will serve up to 100 guests, and bear in mind that the more complicated the design the more expensive the cake will be. If you need to feed a large number of guests your baker can provide extra slices to keep in the kitchen and serve once the main cake has been cut.

Cake styles

The traditional wedding cake is a rich fruit cake, rather like Christmas cake, with marzipan and a coating of royal icing. Your baker may use fondant icing if you want a lot of decoration because it gives a nice smooth surface for moulded flowers, decorations and piped details.

Fruit cake isn't to everyone's taste and there is a trend towards wedding cakes being made from chocolate or flavoured sponge. You can also mix each tier so there is something for everyone. Just remember, if you want to be traditional and keep the top tier for your first child's christening, it needs to be fruit cake since sponge will not keep in the freezer as successfully.

If you are thinking of having an exotically flavoured cake, how about serving it as dessert and cutting your food budget? Once the main course is over you will need to hold the cake-cutting ceremony, then the cake can be sliced and served for pudding. With the addition of ice-cream, cream or a fruity sauce, chocolate cake in particular works perfectly to round off the meal.

Traditional tiers: This is the most formal style of cake where small pillars are set foursquare to support each tier.

American stack: A popular and modern choice where each tier of the cake sits directly on top of the one below with no pillars in between.

Cupcakes: Individual fairy cakes, one for each guest, are piled into a tower on a tiered cake stand. It makes a wonderful centrepiece but does mean you won't be able to have the cake-cutting ceremony.

Croquembouche: A French dessert where cream-filled choux pastry profiteroles are piled into a tower and covered in a rich toffee or chocolate sauce and spun sugar. The bride and groom can cut it in the usual way.

You can display your cake on a small cake table in a corner of the room where it can easily be admired but is not in danger of being knocked over. Once the cake has been cut, sliced and served to your guests, the venue should wrap and re-box any left over, which you will need to arrange to be taken home.

Reception decoration

Your guests spend the majority of the wedding day at the reception venue so it stands to reason you will want to spend most of your decorating budget making the room look as good as possible. How much you have to do will depend on the style of the venue and how much time and money you have to spare, decorating a large room can be expensive.

Hopefully, the basic walls, floor coverings and curtains will be in good decorative order so all you'll need to concentrate on is the entrance and the tables and chairs. You should stick to the theory that less is more and don't get too carried away covering every surface with expensive flowers, balloons, confetti, petals and bows. A few well-placed arrangements and a colour co-ordinated table will look much more effective and won't cost as much.

You usually have the option of round or long tables at most venues – the recent trend is for long tables but it's up to you and the layout of the room. The linens, cutlery and glasses provided by the venue are likely to be pretty standard, with little decoration or individuality. If you want to introduce touches such as coloured glasses, linens or chargers you will have to hire them separately and tell the venue you would rather use these instead.

A clever way of introducing colour to your reception is to use table-runners. This is a strip of coloured fabric draped down the centre of each table and it's a cheap and very effective way of livening up an overly stark all-white look.

Plain or scruffy chairs can easily be covered with chair covers, which you can hire in a variety of colours and fabrics and usually tie with a large bow at the back. They do come at a price but can look very striking and mean you will have to spend less on other decorative touches because you have 100 bow-covered chairs to fill the room.

The seating plan

It probably sounds easy but in fact compiling the seating plan causes many couples considerable headaches, trying to find the best way to deal with dysfunctional families, groups of people who don't know one another, widely different age ranges and people they know won't get along. It's a juggling act of sometimes huge proportions and much as I'd like to tell you that everyone will make an effort to get on on your big day, unfortunately it can't be guaranteed!

The traditional rectangular top table is seated left to right as follows:
Chief bridesmaid, groom's father, bride's mother, groom, bride, bride's father, groom's mother, best man.

If your two sets of parents have never met before you can switch the dads around so that your parents are seated together. If parents are divorced and remarried, it is polite to include their new spouses on the top table, usually sitting next to their partner. If you think there may be ruffled hierarchy feathers, choose a round top table; who is sitting where is then less obvious and it is easier to chat.

If your family situation is very complicated and several members of the main bridal party just don't get along, forget the top table altogether and seat parents with their own family and friends. You can then opt for a top table for just the two of you.

Other tips for a successful seating plan include:

- putting work colleagues together
- putting people with similar interests and of similar ages together
- putting family together (as long as they get along)
- seating your officiant with members of the bridal party, usually your parents
- making a boy-girl-boy-girl arrangement; this tends to work the best and keeps conversation flowing
- putting a single guest who knows nobody on a table with a chatty friend of a similar age or profession and asking him or her to make sure the other guest feels welcome

Tables and favours

A traditional table will be set for anything up to 12 guests with some sort of centrepiece decoration of either fruit or flowers. Keep the centrepieces low so guests can talk over them or high enough that your guests can chat underneath. Each table will usually have one or more printed menus with a list of the food and wines you will be serving.

Whether or not to put a favour at each place setting is up to you and your budget. The traditional five sugared almonds representing health, wealth, fertility, happiness and longevity are often replaced these days with anything from lottery tickets to mini bottles of whisky emblazoned with the wedding date and the happy couple's initials. A token gift to say welcome and thanks for coming is a nice touch but is definitely not necessary or expected.

> ### Real Bride's Hot Tip
> **"***We used strings of white fairy lights from the garden centre to split the food and dancing areas. It looked so pretty once it got dark and lovely in the photographs.***"**
> *Stephanie Miller, London*

You will need to either name or number each table and, unless the wedding is very small, put up a table plan close to the entrance listing the guests seated at each table. A table name or number and a name card on each table for each guest is a must so they can easily find where they should be sitting. It will also make them feel welcome.

The speeches

The thing guaranteed to strike fear into the heart of most men is being asked to make a speech at a wedding. The pressure, particularly on the best man, to deliver a memorable and entertaining ten minutes is huge!

Public speaking isn't for everyone and you need to reassure them that nobody expects an Oscar-winning performance. Sincerity, with the odd funny anecdote if they can manage it, will suffice. Anyone making a speech will need to speak slowly and clearly, projecting their voice so that the guests at the back of the room can hear. Get your groom, dad or best man to practise beforehand with an impartial friend on hand to give an honest appraisal if he is mumbling or racing his words. And if you or your chief bridesmaid are speaking, you should do the same. Suggest that they put key phrases on to cue cards. This usually works better than writing out every word, which would make it too tempting for them to look down the whole time and is likely to make them speak too quickly.

A glass or two of wine for Dutch courage is fine before making a speech; getting drunk is not. If you see your groom or the best man reaching for one too many during the meal, remind them that the speeches are still to come and are likely to be on video for everyone to enjoy for many years! Or, you could have the speeches before the meal to stop people getting so nervous that they can't enjoy their food.

If you are thinking about making a bride's speech – and why not? It is your wedding too – practise what you are going to say at home first. Some brides recite a favourite poem that sums up their feelings towards their husband; other brides have been known to sing a little song; or you may want to tell a funny story about your groom that will make everyone smile.

Ritual humiliation and detailed stories about exes, your sex life or anything else likely to cause any embarrassment should be left to the hen or stag night.

Five tips to keep your guests smiling

1. Set up a wedding website so guests can find venue details, directions, places to stay and gift list information. After the wedding you can post pictures on to the site.
2. Make sure your guests have something to eat and drink while you are having your photos taken. It can take over an hour and they'll be thirsty.
3. Keep everyone in the know about timings – when food will be served, what time the dancing will start, what time the party is due to finish.
4. As far as possible, seat people with people they know. It is good to mingle but pretty boring to be stuck on a table of complete strangers.
5. Plan the dance music carefully and include a good smattering of old favourites that are guaranteed to fill the floor. Have a quiet room where people can go to chat if they want to.

Entertaining ideas

Guests will expect to be provided with some kind of entertainment at a traditional wedding reception. This can take the form of a live band, a disco, a string quartet or recorded music as well as entertainers such as magicians and silhouette artists. As with everything else, it's up to your taste and your budget.

To get everyone into the party mood, a five-piece band is perfect for a smart evening reception in a hotel, whereas a good DJ with a deck is suitable for more informal surroundings such as a marquee. A close-up magician moving from table to table as your guests are eating is always popular. Face painters and even clowns will go down well with your younger guests. If you are hiring any kind of entertainers, make sure you have seen and heard them perform before you book. If they will be providing music it's a good idea to ask for a play list or provide one of your own, bearing in mind that you will need to appeal to all musical tastes and the wide age range of your guests.

Your first dance

All eyes will be on you as you take to the floor so it's worth having a lesson or at least practising a few steps. Stuck for what to play? Here are a few classics:

Beauty and the Beast	Celine Dion and Peabo Bryson
Can You Feel the Love Tonight?	Elton John
Endless Love	Diana Ross and Lionel Richie
Fly Me to the Moon	Frank Sinatra
The First Time Ever I Saw Your Face	Roberta Flack
Forever	Nat King Cole
The Greatest Love of All	Whitney Houston
A Groovy Kind of Love	Phil Collins
How Sweet It Is	James Taylor
I Do	Natalie Cole
It Had To Be You	Harry Connick Jr
My Girl	Temptations
Only You	The Platters
Truly, Madly, Deeply	Savage Garden

Anusha
Dharmasingham
& Tony Stewart

Highclere Castle,
Newbury, Bucks

Chapter *8*

Your Wedding Outfits

This will probably be your favourite chapter because it is all about what you and the rest of the bridal party are going to wear on the big day. Find the low-down on everything from your dream wedding dress and accessories to the perfect suit for your groom.

Every bride is beautiful; perhaps it has something to do with that 'wedding glow' that often descends the week before the big day and lasts until your honeymoon is over. But to make sure you look, as well as feel, beautiful you need to find your dream wedding dress. As special occasions go, your wedding is as big as it gets and you probably won't believe how much time you are going to invest in finding that one perfect dress.

Your wedding dress

Buying a wedding gown is one of life's best shopping experiences. But before rushing out and indulging in a frenzy of trying-on sessions, take some time to look through a few wedding magazines as well as learn a bit of the 'dress lingo'. It will be helpful to everyone if you have at least a vague idea of what you are looking for because there are literally thousands of different options to choose from. You will also need a pretty good idea of your dress budget. You can buy a wedding dress from many different places and can pay anything from a few hundreds to many thousands of pounds.

The bridal shop

This is where you'll find custom-made dresses, and all the big-name bridal designers and manufacturers sell through one or more of these shops. They usually stock a range of bridesmaids' outfits as well as shoes and accessories, so you can buy everything under one roof.

Once you have looked through the latest *You & Your Wedding* magazine you will start to get a feel for the shapes and styles of dress you like. You may also begin to see the same designer names coming up again and again on your favourites lists. Just about all of the big names have a website that not only shows pictures of many, if not all, of the latest collection but also has a list of nationwide stockists. Look at the site to find who stocks a particular designer in your area.

You have to make an appointment to try on a wedding dress in most bridal shops. Don't let this put you off; it's actually for your benefit so you get space in the fitting room and the attention of one of the staff who will be able to advise you on what is available and on things such as fittings and alterations. If possible, try to schedule your first dress shopping day for a weekday rather than a busy Saturday when you may feel a little rushed. It's okay to schedule a couple of appointments in one day but more than three may leave your head spinning, so try to space them out to give yourself some time for reflection.

A dress from a bridal shop is the most expensive option because these shops use the best fabrics and the services of a trained sales person. The dress you ultimately choose will also be made to fit you, which is why you can't just go in and buy 'off the peg' and need to allow anything up to nine months to have the dress made.

> ### Real Bride's Hot Tip
> *66 Don't let the shop assistant bully you when you try on your dress. It's easy to feel intimidated when you're in your knickers. Just remember who is the customer! 99*
> **Jenny Slater, Babbacombe, Devon**

Once you have chosen your dream dress, expect to leave a deposit and schedule a series of fittings appointments. Make sure you find out just what is included in the quoted price; if more alterations need to be made at the last minute because

you have lost weight, for example, you will need to know exactly what this is going to cost. Work out a date when the finished dress will be ready for collection and when the final payment needs to be made.

The high street retailer

You don't have to spend a fortune on your wedding dress and, with most of the major department stores now stocking bridal wear, you can buy a gorgeous dress for a very reasonable price. The fabrics used won't be of the same quality as in many of the specialist bridal shops but if you love the dress and it suits your budget as well as your figure, nobody will be able to tell from your photographs!

If you are a standard size you can probably go in, try on a range of styles and buy a dress on the same day. If the dress needs minor alteration, such as shortening, the shop can probably arrange this for you for a small extra charge. A dress that needs major alteration is probably best avoided, even if you know a good dressmaker. Cheaper dresses are mass-produced, usually in the Far East, and the fabric and seams are not made to be altered; the dress could easily be ruined.

Most bridal wear departments also stock a good range of bridesmaids' dresses and affordable accessories.

The dressmaker

If you have a vision of your perfect dress but the designer prices are just too much, you could get a dressmaker to make it for you. You buy the fabric and between you come up with a design – probably using pictures, with details from one being mixed with details from another. This is not the cheapest option but it will save you a lot on the designer prices. Just be certain that the dressmaker's skills are up to making a wedding dress. It is advisable to see other examples of their work, and be sure that you share the same vision.

Websites

With the rise in popularity of internet shopping, the number of wedding dresses that can be bought on the web has increased. Sites such as eBay are brimming with everything from gowns to tiaras, veils and shoes at seemingly great prices. But it can be a risky process; many of the dresses will be shipped from the Far East, so you need to be sure of what you are ordering before parting with your money. Most website sellers don't offer refunds. Anyone who is a standard size 8–14 may be lucky; however this is not the route to take if you are not a typical shape.

Real Bride's Hot Tip
❝ *Wedding shows are a great place to see lots of dresses under one roof. I had never heard of many of the designers and found my dress in one afternoon!* **❞**
Colleen Joseph, Billericay Essex

Sample sales

All designers hold regular sample sales, usually at the end of each season, when they sell off old stock and the shop samples at greatly reduced prices. Keep an eye on individual designer's websites and ask the shops for dates of expected sales. Again if you are a standard size 8–12 you can pick up an amazing bargain. The dresses are likely to be a bit dirty but some of what you save can be put towards specialist cleaning.

Vintage dresses

Wearing your mother's wedding dress is guaranteed to add a very personal touch to your day – providing you are much the same size and the style of the dress can be subtly updated. Alternatively, keep an eye out at charity shops for vintage dresses. There are even several Oxfam shops in England with special bridal departments. As long as the fabric is still in good condition and you have a clever seamstress friend you could have a unique dress at a fabulous price.

Taking the fashion option

If you chose a more informal, contemporary wedding, there's nothing to say you can't ignore the whole bridal industry and choose any dress you love. You can buy an appropriate mid-length or evening dress from one of the mainstream designer's latest collections for the same price, or cheaper, than many wedding dresses.

Dress shopping tips

Shop only with people whose opinions you trust. Limit the shopping party to four including you.

Feel free to shop on your own for the first couple of appointments, inviting mothers and maids once you have a shortlist.

Wear supportive lingerie and take along a strapless bra and a pair of shoes with roughly the heel height you think you'll be wearing on the day.

Keep your budget in mind and don't try on dresses out of your price range.

Try on a variety of styles. Many have little hanger-appeal but look great on.

Even if you spend a long time in one shop, don't feel you have to buy.

If one dress is not quite right, ask if the same designer has a similar style, perhaps with a different neckline or sleeves that you may like better. Shops won't stock every style but they may be able to get something for you.

Take advice from the sales person – but don't be bullied. If you don't like something, it's thanks but no thanks!

Don't buy on your first shopping trip. You can always go back if you have been lucky enough to have found 'the one' first time out!

Shapes and silhouettes

It's a good idea to learn a little about the various styles of wedding dresses before you start shopping, so you know what that sales person is talking about.

Dress shapes

A-line: The most flattering style so it's no surprise that this is the most popular shape of wedding gown. The dress gently flares out from the shoulders and suits most figure shapes and heights.

Ballgown: The ultimate fairytale dress with a narrow fitted waistline and a full, flowing skirt. It's a 'big' dress so tends to suit taller girls.

Empire: Cut a bit like a maternity dress with a high waistline that starts just below the bust. The skirt is usually slim and flowing. Avoid this shape if you have a very full bust; you don't want to look pregnant.

Princess: Another popular shape that suits most figure types. Vertical panels of fabric follow the natural contours of the body to give a flattering outline.

Sheath: Simple and elegant, this style of dress follows the natural curves from shoulder to hem. They are usually in fabrics that tend to cling so don't really suit either very slender or very curvy figures.

Length options

Asymmetric: This style of skirt features one side longer than the other. It's a dramatic look and suits a contemporary wedding.

Ballerina: A ballerina skirt finishes just above your ankles and is wide and full. It is a pretty, traditional style that demands great shoes!

Cocktail: This style of skirt finishes just below the knee. It's an informal look that is best suited to a register office or a second wedding.

Floor-length: The classic length for a wedding dress, which finishes about 3 cm / 1 ¼ in from the floor.

Mini: If you are thinking about changing after the formal part of the day is over, a thigh-skimming dress is great for a party, providing you have good legs.

Preserving your wedding dress

You'll want to keep your wedding dress in the best possible condition so have it dry cleaned by a specialist cleaner as soon as possible after the wedding, pointing out any stains when you take it in. The best way to store your dress is to pack it in acid-free tissue paper and put it into a box away from light and insects.

A-line

Ballgown

Empire

Princess

Sheath

Asymmetric

Ballerina

Cocktail

Floor-length

Mini

Bridal accessories

Once you have found your perfect dress you will want to think about accessories. A headdress, veil, shoes and lingerie are all important parts of putting together a total look.

The headdress

Most brides will want to wear something in their hair and if you are wearing a veil you'll need some sort of accessory on which to secure it. There are lots of options from the plain to full-on glamour.

Alice band: Plain or decorated with a bow or pearls, this is a simple, easy-to-wear accessory that looks pretty and modern without being overly fussy.

Clips and combs: Ideal if you want a little decoration but nothing too fancy. They can be used to secure an up-do or a veil. Usually decorated with diamanté or pearls but you can choose whatever style you like.

Crown: A must for any fairytale bride but they can be tricky to keep on and you might need professional help to pin it securely.

Hat: For an informal wedding, particularly in a register office, a hat is a stylish option and they are perfect if you are wearing a simple dress and hate the thought of a veil.

Tiara: This is the classic bridal headdress and works with any style of dress and just about any hairstyle, up or down. Choose from simple bands to ornate creations. Just make sure it fits your head snugly so it doesn't keep slipping forwards. You don't want to spend the day worried that it's about to drop off.

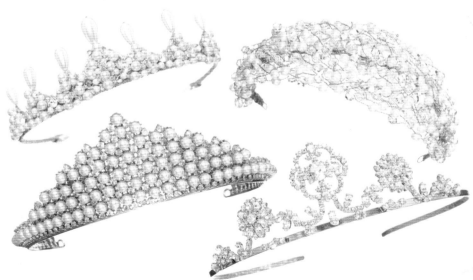

The veil

The veil goes in and out of fashion but for a traditional bride is a must-have on her wedding day. Buy your veil once you have found your dress, perhaps reflecting one or more of its details, such as a lace edge or pearl trim. Choose your veil from a variety of different styles in traditional tulle, luxurious lace or elegant silk chiffon.

Ballet: A floor length veil made of several simple layers, often worn very long to double-up as a train.

Blusher: A short, usually single-layer veil that reaches to the shoulders. It often comes attached to a hair comb.

Fingertip: Probably the most popular choice, with several layers of fabric extending to the fingertips.

Mantilla: A traditional Spanish-inspired lace veil that's worn without a headdress and is simply draped over the head to frame the face.

Waterfall: A very romantic look, with several layers of veiling attached to a hair band that cascades down to the hip or knees. The top layer is often short so it can easily be turned back once you reach the altar.

Wedding shoes

A great pair of wedding shoes will have you walking on air but they have to be comfortable too; you could be standing for anything up to ten hours! If you are

not used to wearing high heels, your wedding day isn't the time to start. A two-inch heel is the most comfortable height and will work with most styles of dress.

Choose your shoes before any final fittings for your dress to ensure the heel height works with the length of the dress. Many bridal shops keep a range of shoes with varying heels for you wear when trying on a dress, but for final fittings you will want to have your own shoes with you.

Once you have bought your wedding shoes, wear them around the house a few times to get used to them and scuff the soles so you don't slip – a potential problem if your venue has shiny wooden floors.

Bridal lingerie

A well-fitting set of lingerie can make all the difference to how your dress looks so it is important to choose something that's comfortable but also works with the style of your gown. Try several styles with your chosen dress and move around, trying out a few dance steps to make sure it all feels comfortable and stays hidden.

Bra Just about any style of wedding dress will look better worn with a bra. Even if your dress has skinny straps, a low back or is strapless, there are plenty of suitable bras that will give you invisible support. If you are less well-endowed you may like to try a push-up bra to boost your cleavage – and you can buy minimiser bras to make less of more. If your dress is very low-cut and you are small-busted you can probably get away with using bra tape – a flesh-coloured tape that you stick on to your skin – for a little extra support.

Bustier A long-line alternative to a bra, often sold in the bridal shops, which comes down to the top of your knickers and can be used with stockings. They are usually quite heavily boned and offer good support for the fuller figure, but they can also be quite restricting so make sure you will feel comfortable all day.

Bodyshaper A little bit of Lycra is a great idea if you want to create a smooth silhouette and look a couple of pounds lighter. This style of pants is a lot more comfortable than anything your mother might have worn but the restrictive fabric still gets some getting used to. Wear them a couple of times before the wedding just to be sure you are happy.

Knickers and thongs Whatever style of pants you wear, functionality is much more important than whether they look sexy. Plain knickers are less likely to show than anything decorated with ribbons and bows, however pretty. And flesh-coloured underwear is often a better choice than white.

Hosiery Tights, stockings or hold-ups? The choice is yours but, again, comfort is the most important factor. You don't want to spend the day with your thighs being constricted by overly tight hold-ups any more than you want to be hitching up sagging stockings. The most flattering wedding hosiery is a natural or nude shade rather than white. And don't forget the garter!

Wedding rings

Your wedding band will probably become your most important piece of jewellery since it symbolises the moment you became man and wife. You may have chosen this ring at the same time as your engagement ring or you may be buying it just before the wedding.

When you choose your wedding ring, always wear your engagement ring so you know that they'll fit neatly together and feel comfortable. If you have a gold engagement ring you are most likely to choose a hard-wearing 18ct gold band: if your engagement ring is platinum you will need to buy a platinum band. Weddings bands are traditionally plain but many modern styles incorporate diamonds – lovely if your budget allows!

Allow enough time before the wedding to get your ring (or rings if your groom wants to wear one) engraved with your initials, the wedding date or a simple love note to one another.

Something old, something new…

…something borrowed, something blue and a silver sixpence in her shoe. This is an old English rhyme meant to bring good luck to the bride and you too will probably want to carry on this tradition on your wedding day.

Something old that you can take from the past into your new life. A piece of family jewellery or an inherited Bible or book of poems is often used.

Something new to celebrate your new married life. Just about everything you will be wearing will be new so this one is easy!

Something borrowed is usually taken from a happily married friend in the hope that some of their good fortune will rub off on you. A handkerchief, earrings or a bracelet are popular choices.

Something blue, the colour of fidelity. Blue coloured flowers in your bouquet, a blue bow on your garter, or sapphire earrings (which could be borrowed as well and do both jobs!).

Bridesmaids' outfits

The good news for you and your prospective maids is that fashion has finally caught up with the bridesmaid dress and you will be able to choose from many gorgeous styles that look more like party dresses than the frilly nightmares from days gone by. You may be able to buy your bridesmaids' dresses from the same place as your wedding gown. Otherwise check out department stores for reasonably priced ideas – without dismissing the evening wear section, which may have just what you are looking for.

Your maids are bound to be different ages, shapes and sizes and it's perfectly acceptable to let them wear similar but not identical dresses. As long as the colour and the length are the same you'll achieve a well co-ordinated look. It's important that your maids feel comfortable with what they are wearing and it is very difficult to find one dress that suits everyone.

Modern bridesmaids will be spoilt for choice of style as well as colour. Dresses can be long or knee-length (no shorter) but tend to be fairly plain without much decorative detailing. Empire-line or sheath shapes work well and can be teamed with a bolero or wrap in cooler weather. When it comes to colour, choose whatever works with the theme of the day. Bridesmaids' dresses come in every shade from pastels to black. Floral fabrics are a popular choice, particularly in the summer.

Bridesmaids' accessories tend to be simple, perhaps an Alice band or a floral hair comb. It looks really good if all your maids wear the same style of shoes, which can be dyed to match the dresses by many of the specialist shoe companies.

Ideally you should choose your bridesmaids' dresses about six months before the wedding, after you have finalised your own dress. It's traditional for your maids to pay for their own outfits, so do bear this in mind when you are shopping. It is fine for you to have your say but if you fall in love with a particularly expensive style you may need to offer to make a contribution towards the cost. Bridesmaids usually carry a simple posy of fresh flowers as well.

Junior attendants

Little bridesmaids, flower girls and page boys need to look cute but feel comfortable in what they are wearing, otherwise you are in for a troubled event. It's usual for the bride to make suggestions about the general style and colour she would like smaller attendants to wear but, since their parents will be footing the bill, you'll need to get their input too before making any final decisions. And it would be sensible to wait until only three or so months before the wedding as small children can have surprising – and inconvenient – growth spurts!

Little girls Young bridesmaids and flower girls should echo the colour scheme and general look of the older maids. White dresses are the most popular choice, with a coloured sash and trimmings in the wedding theme. Other options are velvet for a winter wedding or a pinafore dress for a summer wedding. Bridesmaids' dresses can be pricey, particularly when bought from a bridal boutique, so don't forget to look in the local children's wear shops and at department store collections.

Little boys The traditional outfits for page boys and ring bearers are velvet suits with short trousers, a jacket and a white shirt. This is okay for very small boys but you'll probably have trouble persuading your footie-mad cousins aged six and over to even try on such an outfit! Most young boys will feel happier in a scaled-down version of what the rest of the men in the bridal party will be wearing. Many formal wear shops offer suits in tiny sizes and there is something very cute about youngsters in this style of dress.

Mothers of the bride and groom

It is a big day for both the mothers in the bridal party and they will want to dress to impress. There's lots of choice and to a certain extent what they wear will be dictated by the formality of the wedding. A shift dress with a matching coat, a coatdress, or a longer dress teamed with a little jacket are all popular styles. A softly tailored trouser suit in a pastel shade is acceptable at all but the most formal of weddings. Most mothers will also want to wear some sort of hat or at least one of the latest headdresses adorned with feathers in a complementary colour to her outfit.

It's usual for the mother of the bride to tell the groom's mother the colour and general style of her outfit before the wedding. This is not to say that they have to follow the same style of dress; the most important thing is that they both feel comfortable and confident in what they are wearing.

Your mum may feel that her hair and make-up could do with updating and what better excuse than a wedding to splash out on a little pampering? Think about booking a mother-and-daughter day at your local spa or beauty salon. It would be a good chance to relax and chat and could give your mum a real confidence boost before the big day.

Your groom's outfit

Rightly or wrongly, the groom's outfit won't generate much interest at the wedding; all eyes will be on you and the dress you are wearing. That's not to say that his outfit is unimportant; every groom will want to feel confident in his choice of suit and, since his outfit dictates what the rest of the men in the main bridal party will wear, he needs to set the right tone.

Morning wear This is the most popular choice for the groom, traditionally consisting of grey striped trousers, a black, grey or navy single-breasted tailcoat, wing-collar shirt, waistcoat, silk tie or cravat and sometimes a top hat. It is a traditional look that suits church and more formal civil ceremonies. Morning wear can be given a more modern look if you chose matching trousers and jacket and the addition of a patterned waistcoat and a plain-collar shirt.

Frock coat Frock coats can be plain, patterned brocade, velvet or silk and generally reach down to mid-thigh with a standard or Nehru-style collar. They are worn with plain black trousers, a white shirt and cravat and are a modern alternative to morning wear that can be worn at all but the most formal weddings.

Highland dress Scottish grooms will cut a stylish dash in Highland morning or evening dress, including a kilt, Prince Charlie jacket or doublet, a sporran, laced brogues, bow tie, socks and *sgian dubh* – a small dagger worn in the sock.

Military uniform If the groom is a full-time member of the armed forces, he will usually wear his dress uniform to his wedding.

Lounge suit At a contemporary, usually civil, wedding, your groom may feel more comfortable wearing a lounge suit. This is his chance to splash out on a designer suit from one of the latest collections. The safest colour choices are still black or navy, though cream suits are popular at summer weddings.

Black tie Black tie is a glamorous choice for a wedding and consists of a tuxedo, white shirt and a black bow tie. It is most suited to a late afternoon ceremony and evening wedding reception in formal surroundings. If the main bridal party is in black tie it follows that the rest of the male guests should wear it too, with the women in evening gowns, and you should specify 'black tie' on the invitations.

Groom's accessories

This may be the first time in his life that your groom has had to think about accessories but it's not as daunting as it sounds. The main options include:

Waistcoat Usually the groom and his attendants wear matching waistcoats that complement the colour scheme of the wedding. Waistcoats come in lots of different designs and range from the traditional plain to the brightly coloured. It's traditional to leave the bottom button undone.

Tie There are three main choices: the standard tie, which can be knotted in different ways depending on the size of knot you want; the cravat, which is normally worn with morning wear; and the bow tie, usually worn at more formal evening celebrations.

Cufflinks These should be chosen to suit the formality of a wedding – they are available in just about every style and colour imaginable. Your groom can buy personalised cufflinks for a more individual touch, adding the wedding date, the word 'groom' or even a picture of the bride!

Hat Top hats are not as popular as they once were but if he wants to look super-smart it does complete the formal wear style – even though the groom won't usually wear the topper but just carry it in his left hand. The most usual option would be to hire a hat along with the rest of his outfit.

Buy or hire?

Unless your groom goes to lots of weddings and would get the wear out of his own morning suit, the groom and the rest of the main bridal party are most likely to hire their suits. It is best to organise the hire of the suits at least two months before the big day, particularly if you are marrying in the peak wedding season between June and September.

Once the groom has chosen the style for his suit and the colour and design for accessories such as the waistcoat and cravat, he needs to let the rest of his groomsmen – and both fathers – know his choice so they can all arrange for a fitting. Most hire companies will have your suits ready about a week before the wedding so you can have a final fitting and check that everyone has the right size. Don't leave the final fitting until the day before the wedding; there may not be time to make any last-minute adjustments. The best man should take charge of ensuring that all the ushers have organised their suits in plenty of time.

Hired outfits are normally returned the first working day after the wedding and, again, this is generally a job for the best man – since the groom will almost certainly be on his honeymoon. Most hire companies offer an accidental damage waiver, which is definitely worthwhile in case of mishaps, particularly when the drink is flowing!

If your groom decides to buy a suit for his wedding, he should still start looking at least two months in advance so that any fitting adjustments can be made in plenty of time. The groom usually lets other members of the bridal party know well in advance what colour suit he will be wearing and the level of formality. If he's wearing a lounge suit, you won't want the dads and uncles turning up in morning wear.

Your Wedding Outfits

135

*Aki Yoshimura
& Paul Myers*

*Le Manoir Aux Quat'
Saisons, Oxfordshire*

Chapter 9

Your Wedding Stationery

Your invitations will give your guests their first indication not only of the where, when and how but also the whole style of the day. Formal, funky or fun, use the same design to tie the day together from the order of service through to the place cards at the reception.

Just about anything goes when it comes to modern wedding stationery, from the traditional embossed white board to a funky, hand-decorated card that oozes fun and romance. But before you get too carried away, remember that the invitation is first and foremost a functional item. It needs to clearly relay when, where and how the festivities are taking place. It usually includes the names of the hosts, the names of the bride and groom, the wedding date, timings and address of the ceremony and/or reception plus how to RSVP (unless you enclose separate reply cards).

Invitations are normally sent out between two and three months before the wedding date, allowing a little longer if you are marrying in the traditionally popular holiday months of July and August or around Christmas when potential guests may have commitments of their own or be away.

Spend some time investigating different options. Most of the high street department stores and major stationers offer a wedding stationery service, and there's a host of specialist stationery companies offering thousands of different styles.

Most of the bigger companies carry a set number of designs – which don't vary hugely from company to company – and you can choose the lettering style to go inside. If you want something personalised or unusual you will probably have to check out a specialist wedding stationer, which is likely to be more expensive but you will get something individual.

Invitation styles

You want to choose your invitations to reflect the type of wedding you are planning. Traditionally the plainer and more traditional the invitation, the more formal the wedding. But before making your final choice, think about the following:

The wedding style A black tie wedding demands a traditional invitation, whereas a more relaxed invitation would perfectly suit a contemporary civil wedding. Your guests will take their cue on how much (or how little) to dress up from your invitations.

Colour scheme If you are having a strong colour theme throughout the wedding, use this on your invitations. If butterflies or fairies are a big part of your day, make them a big part of the invitations too.

Your personal taste If you are known as a fun-loving couple, then your guests may think a traditional invitation isn't exactly your style. Everything about your wedding should be a reflection of the two of you.

The number of guests A small wedding means you can indulge in pricier invitations, perhaps having something hand-made. If you are having many guests, or need to include a lot of other information such as a map, hotel information and parking details in the same envelope, plain and simple is probably your best bet.

Printing styles

The price of invitations varies as much as the styles and depends very much on where you buy from. If you are particularly adept with a PC you could make your own invitations using a computer graphics package.

Engraving This is the most expensive form of printing and is used for ultra-formal invitations. It involves using a metal plate engraved with the words, which stamps them on to the paper from the back, giving them a raised appearance on the front of the card.

Thermography The most popular method used by the big stationery companies and it looks much like engraving; the only real way to tell is that the back of the letters will feel smooth (engraved lettering has been pushed into the paper). The price will also tell you it's not engraving – thermography is a much cheaper option for a formal-looking invitation.

Embossing This is another expensive technique that makes individual, larger letters raised and shiny. It's often used for the couple's initials or for a border and is perfect if you want your invitations to look extra special.

Offset printing This is the most cost-effective method of printing and is used for all sorts of cards, letterheads and posters. It also offers the most flexibility for contemporary invitations using different papers, including decoration, coloured inks and photographs.

Calligraphy The age-old art of handwriting – pretty and expensive if done by a calligraphy specialist because each invitation is hand written. But there are computer packages that can reproduce the look.

At the same time as ordering your invitations, order a set of matching envelopes, with plenty of spares to allow for mistakes. The latest designs have coloured tissue inserts that can be matched to your colour theme.

Invitation wording

The invitation traditionally comes from whoever is hosting the wedding; often this is the bride's parents but it could be the groom's parents or, more likely these days, the couple themselves. If you are stuck for what to say, ask your stationer for advice – they'll have seen every permutation going at some stage – and don't be afraid to adapt traditional wording to suit your family circumstances.

Bride's parents as wedding hosts

Mr and Mrs Paul Smith
request the pleasure of your company
at the marriage of their daughter
Suzanne Amanda
and
Michael John Peters
3.00pm Saturday 20th June 2007
at St Mary's Church, Amberley
and afterwards for dinner and dancing in
The Purcell Suite, The Red Lion Hotel,
Amberley, Sussex
RSVP to Mrs Paul Smith, [insert telephone number], by 10th May 2007
(you can request the honour of your guests' company if the style is very formal)

Couple hosting their own wedding

Ms Suzanne Amanda Smith
and
Mr Michael John Peters
request the pleasure of your company
at their marriage
3.00pm Saturday 20th June 2007
at St Mary's Church, Amberley
and afterwards for dinner and dancing in
The Purcell Suite, The Red Lion Hotel,
Amberley, Sussex
RSVP to Colette Smith, [insert telephone number], by 10th May 2007

Single or widowed parent hosting the wedding

Mr Paul Smith
requests the pleasure of your company
at the marriage of his daughter
Suzanne Amanda Smith
to
Michael John Peters
3.00pm Saturday 20th June 2007

at St Mary's Church, Amberley
and afterwards for dinner and dancing in
The Purcell Suite, The Red Lion Hotel,
Amberley, Sussex
RSVP to Colette Smith, [insert telephone number], by 10th May 2007

Divorced parents hosting the wedding

Mr Paul Smith and Mrs Claire Jones
request the pleasure of your company
at the marriage of their daughter
Suzanne Amanda Smith
to
Michael John Peters
3.00pm Saturday 20th June 2007
at St Mary's Church, Amberley
and afterwards for dinner and dancing in
The Purcell Suite, The Red Lion Hotel,
Amberley, Sussex
RSVP Mrs Claire Jones, [insert telephone number], by 10th May 2007

Divorced and remarried parent hosting the wedding

Mr Paul Smith and Mrs Vanessa Brown
request the pleasure of your company
at the marriage of Mr Smith's daughter
Suzanne Amanda Smith
to
Michael John Peters
3.00pm Saturday 20th June 2007
at St Mary's Church, Amberley
and afterwards for dinner and dancing in
The Purcell Suite, The Red Lion Hotel,
Amberley, Sussex
RSVP Mrs Vanessa Brown, [insert telephone number], by 10th May 2007

It is usual to leave a space within the invitation to write in the guests' names or to write their names in the top right hand corner. Either way, this needs to be done well, preferably using black ink. If neither you and your groom nor a friend has good enough handwriting you could invest in a professional calligrapher to do the job. Most stationers will know someone, otherwise look in the Yellow Pages.

Finishing touches

Stationery is expensive and you don't want to make any costly mistakes. Check and double check all the details before giving the printer the go-ahead. It is a good idea to get someone not closely involved with your plans, such as a work colleague, to do the final proofreading. He or she might well spot something that you have overlooked – such as the time or wedding date – which is easier to leave off than you might imagine! Check all spellings carefully and be quite sure that you like the layout and the typeface and that it reflects the style of the day. Keep a copy of the marked proof showing any corrections you make, then recheck everything when you collect the stationery. Printers make mistakes too and you should ideally sort out any hiccups before leaving the shop.

If you are using a mail order service, make sure you receive a sample of the exact paper they'll be using and any envelopes before you place the final order. There are so many different papers available that vary in colour, weight and texture and you'll want to be certain you have ordered the right one for you.

Informal invitations

If you are having an informal wedding, there's no reason why the invitation wording shouldn't reflect the occasion.

- Suzanne and Michael are tying the knot. Join us for a drink (or two) at The Red Lion Hotel…
- Suzanne and Michael invite you to join them and celebrate their union…
- We're getting hitched! Join Suzanne and Michael to celebrate their marriage…
- Suzanne and Michael are finally getting hitched! We would love you to join us and celebrate our marriage on Saturday 20 June…
- Love is in the air! Join Suzanne and Michael to celebrate their marriage…

Always order more invitations than you think you'll need, at least an extra 20 to allow for mistakes and to invite last-minute guests. You should expect about 5 per cent of your 'A-list' guests to be unable to come. You will also want to keep a couple of invitations in your wedding album.

Give the task of monitoring the RSVP list to a trusted relative or friend. This is often a job either mother will relish; put their contact details at the bottom of the invitation with a 'reply by' date if you like. The chances are most guests will reply within a fortnight but some may need chasing up. Alternatively, you may like to enclose reply cards and addressed envelopes with the invitations. This is the most formal option and pricey for you, since it's expected that you put a stamp on the envelope for your guests to use as well!

Additional wedding stationery

At the same time as looking for invitations, you should think about the other stationery you may need for the wedding. It will give the most co-ordinated look to use the same design and type style for all your stationery.

Save-the-date cards These are always recommended if you are marrying during the summer months or close to Christmas when many of your guests may be planning holidays or celebrations of their own. It just needs to be a simple card saying something like:

Suzanne and Michael are getting married. Please save 20th June 2007 for our wedding celebrations. Invitation to follow soon.

Invitation reply cards These are sent out with the invitations and are a good idea if you think your guests may be slow to respond to a telephone number or email address. One of the things you won't want to be worrying about is exactly who is going to show up at your wedding! A 'delete where appropriate' format is usually the best:

Suzanne and Michael's wedding
[blank space for the guests' names] *would be delighted to accept/*
unfortunately cannot accept your kind invitation for 20th June 2007.

You will need to include a stamped addressed envelope with the reply card, or you could make it a stamped addressed postcard to save on the cost of another envelope.

Order of service

This is like a programme or running order for the ceremony part of your wedding, either put on to each person's chair or handed out by the ushers as guests arrive at the ceremony. The order of service details everything involved in the ceremony from the arrival of the bride through to the recessional as the couple leave the ceremony as man and wife.

It is usual to include the names of the couple and the celebrant, all the words for each of the hymns, details of the readings and the names of the people giving them, and the name of the organist if you are having one. It is supposed to be a useful document but is very personal as well so feel free to include special tributes to absent, perhaps deceased, relatives and thank yous for special friends who have contributed in some extra way to your day. Before ordering, make sure you check all the proposed details with your celebrant. You'll need his or her agreement to all hymns and readings before you can go ahead.

As with other stationery, check and double check all texts before printing. Order enough order of service sheets to allow one for each guest plus an additional 20 copies to account for any unexpected people who may come along to the ceremony to wish you well.

Reception stationery

While none of the following is an essential part of your wedding, they do make it simpler for your guests to find their seats and to feel welcomed to your party. None of these have to be costly but they will help to set the right celebratory tone. You can get your designated stationery company to make them as part of the stationery order; otherwise you can easily make simple versions on a computer and print them out yourselves.

Table plan Usually sited just outside the entrance to the reception, mounted on a board and displayed on a painter's easel. The type used needs to be big enough that guests can see their names easily. Put the name or number of the table followed by a list of the names seated at that table.

Place cards Once your guests find their allocated table, it is a nice touch to find their name on a card sitting on their plate. These can be simple cards or more elaborate ideas like threading them on to a ribbon for hanging on each chair.

Menu Your guests will want to know what they are eating so a menu card in the centre of each table will be most welcome. Indicate any vegetarian options and give the name and vintage of each of the wines you have chosen.

Thank you cards Your guests will expect to receive a thank you card for their wedding gift. These can either be sent out as and when you receive each gift or you can do them all in one go after the honeymoon is over. It is nice to keep the wedding style going and have thank you cards printed using the same design as your other stationery. Alternatively, you might like to have one of your favourite wedding pictures turned into a simple card.

Hand write the cards (a printed card is not considered polite) and mention the gift and perhaps how you may be using it in the future. Nobody expects a work of art; just a few heartfelt words of thanks is fine.

Cancelling a wedding

This is not something any couple will want to think about but circumstances do sometimes dictate cancellation or postponement and, if time allows, it is best to do this in writing. It also avoids having to make painful phone calls if the wedding has been called off due to the death of a close relative or because of cold feet.

Mr and Mrs John Smith
announce that the marriage of
their daughter
Suzanne Amanda
to
Michael John Peters
will not now take place/has been postponed

There's no need to go into details on this type of card, though you can include a personal note to close friends and relatives if you feel more information is necessary.

*Hollie Clarke
& James Kebell*

*Babington House,
Somerset*

Chapter 10

Your Flowers

A wedding wouldn't be a wedding without beautiful flowers. Use them to colour co-ordinate the whole day, providing a gorgeous backdrop for both your ceremony and your reception. Even a few flowers can tranform a room, delighting your guests with their wonderful fragrance.

Flowers play a big part in any wedding and whether your budget is big or small you'll want to include some flowers in your celebrations. Your first step towards floral perfection is to find a florist. Flowers set the style for the whole day so this is an all-important partnership. You are looking for someone in tune with what you like who will bring a sense of style and drama to the occasion.

Choosing a florist

The florist is one of your most important wedding suppliers and you should expect to visit at least three to discuss your ideas and compare prices. The trick is to find a florist who can make your dreams come true, without blowing your budget.

Look through magazines to find florists in the area close to the wedding venue and ask for recommendations from friends and other suppliers such as the venue or photographer. Make appointments with your shortlist of favourites, avoiding Saturday if possible when the shop is more likely to be busy and staff may not be able to give you their full attention. Arm yourself with details of your wedding, the date, the venue, pictures of your dress, fabric samples and some idea of flowers that you like. You also need to have a clear idea of how much you have to spend. As a rough guide, 5 per cent of your total budget is about average.

At your initial meeting, it's also quite usual to take along pictures of arrangements you like. You won't be expected to know the names of all the flowers, but pictures will give the florist a good idea of the type of flowers you like as well as a general insight into how you see the overall colour and style of the day.

Any good florist should be able to come up with designs you like to suit your wedding without blowing your budget. Be prepared to listen to their ideas; they may need to adapt your initial thoughts to achieve something that works for the money. And you need to allow them room for creativity. They are the experts after all!

You can book your florist anything up to a year in advance and you should expect to pay a small deposit at the time of booking. Visit the venue together and start firming up details two to three months before the wedding, finalising your choices about three weeks before the big day.

What flowers do you need?

Make a list of all the areas in your wedding where you would like to include flowers. Try to visualise the ceremony room, reception venue, your bouquet, your

Questions to ask your florist

❏ Have you worked at my venue before?

❏ Do you have photos of your work, especially weddings at my venue?

❏ Which flowers will be in season?

❏ How can I make the most of my budget?

❏ Do you have things such as vases and candelabra to hire or buy?

❏ Will you personally be doing my flowers or will it be one of your colleagues?

❏ When do I have to finalise my flower choices?

❏ What is the timetable for the flowers on the wedding day?

❏ Do I need to leave a deposit at the time of booking? When will the balance be due?

bridesmaids' flowers, buttonholes and other accessories. Write down the ideal flower requirements for each part of the day so you can chat your ideas through with your florist.

If you are having a church wedding, the church may have its own florist or you may decide to use your own. Think about having pedestal arrangements at the altar where all eyes will be focused and, if your budget allows it, a small floral arrangement at the end of each pew. Decorating the entrance to the church is a popular idea since this is where many of your photographs will be taken. Providing paper cones of fresh or freeze-dried petals for your guests to use as confetti is another nice idea you may like to consider.

If you are having a civil wedding it's popular to have a pedestal arrangement or large table centrepiece where you say your vows. Once this part of the day is over, the flowers can be moved into the reception area, instantly halving that particular cost. At a register office ceremony, some sort of floral arrangement will already be in the marriage room and, since the ceremony is so quick, most couples don't bother adding personal touches, preferring to use their budget at the reception where their guests will be spending the most time.

First impressions count, so the entrance to the reception room should be welcoming, drawing your guests inside. This is the place for an impressive pedestal or a floral door wreath, perhaps with ribbon bearing your names and the wedding date. You could also drape a length of tulle (a lightweight, very fine netting) around the door frame and secure it with flowers in the top corners – inexpensive and very striking!

Keep your table arrangements either low, no more than 25 cm/10 in high, so your guests can talk over them, or in tall vases so that they can talk under them. A guest who has to spend several hours facing a lot of flowers (however lovely), left out of the conversation on the other side of the table, will feel rather disappointed. You can also incorporate flowers as place markers; tie a simple name tag on to the stem of a single flower, or tie a small posy on the back of each chair to welcome your guests to the table.

Some couples like to have a very small fresh flower arrangement on top of the wedding cake instead of the traditional mini bride and groom figures.

The groom usually presents the mother of the bride and his own mother, and also anyone who has contributed to the wedding in a special way (did a friend or relative make the cake, for instance?), with a bouquet or a flower arrangement during his speech.

Seasons and colours
Perfect colour combinations, whatever the time of the year.

Spring
Pastel pink and white
Lemon yellow and white
Gold and ivory

Summer
Yellow and mint green
Cool white
Tiffany blue and silver

Autumn
Orange and gold
Lilac and white
Gold and cream

Winter
Ice white
Silver and white
Red and rich green

Colour schemes

While the main aim is to choose flowers in a colour that you like, there are other factors to take into consideration before making your final choices. Think about where you will be holding your ceremony and reception. You want to create a feeling of relaxation and harmony so the décor and the flowers have to work together. If, for example, you love delicate, pastel pink flowers but your reception venue has a heavily patterned carpet and brocade curtains, you may have to rethink what flowers you use in that room. The answer could be to have a pastel pink bouquet but stronger-coloured flowers for the table centrepieces. This is why it's important to work with a florist who has either already done a wedding at your venue or at least visited the venue, so he or she knows exactly what it looks like as they make suggestions.

The simplest solution to setting a theme is to go with the season. This will also help your budget since abundant seasonal flowers will be cheaper than imported or specially grown flowers that are not usually available at that time of the year. For instance, spring and summer weddings work best with pastel flowers and lots of white, while an autumn or winter wedding, when it is likely to be dark, allows you to choose brighter, bolder colours.

Real Bride's Hot Tip

66 There were three weddings on the same day at our church so I got together with the other brides and we all used the same flowers and split the cost.99

Samantha Darrow,
Uxbridge, Middlesex

Ask your florist about incorporating colour in the form of beads, feathers and other fabrics in the table arrangements and your bouquet. This is currently very popular and works particularly well with a contemporary theme.

Style on a budget

Creating a floral extravaganza with a large budget is easy but if you don't have a lot to spend you shouldn't have to compromise on style, just be a little more creative. Be honest with your florist from day one about your budget so he or she knows what is available to work with.

Obviously, the easiest way to save money is to have fewer flowers – particularly ornate, time-consuming table arrangements – but there are other ways to save

money. If there is a particular flower that you love but it is proving expensive, use it sparingly – perhaps only in your bridal bouquet, making it doubly special and even more memorable. There is nothing to say that all your flowers have to be the same; providing the overall colour scheme works you should feel free to mix and match. Don't dismiss 'common' flowers either as they can look stunning in the creative hands of a good florist. Carnations, tulips and daffodils are all inexpensive and look beautiful when used massed into large vases.

Other ways of saving money include using the ceremony flowers at your reception. There's usually at least an hour or two before guests come into the dining room when larger arrangements can be moved. It is also worth asking if there are other weddings being held in your church on the same day as you may be able to split the cost of the flowers with the other couples.

If you are thinking about having quite simple flower arrangements, speak to the church flower arrangers and see if the reception venue has an on-site florist. Both will probably do a great job and save you money. If your wedding is close to Christmas or Easter, ask how it will be decorated – you may be able to work your colour scheme around the flowers that will already be there.

Surprisingly few flowers need to be used to make a visual statement and fill a room with fragrance. Ask your florist about using lilies, hyacinths, frangipani, apple and orange blossom, mimosa, stocks, jasmine and sweet peas in some of the reception arrangements. All of these have a beautiful scent.

And don't think you have to cover every surface with flowers. Often less is more and a few tall, striking arrangements, well placed where your guests will see them, work better than lots of smaller arrangements on each table.

The bride's bouquet

The bouquet is the ultimate wedding accessory, your options being limited only by the availability of the flowers and the skill of the florist. The style of the wedding and the shape of your dress will guide you towards the perfect bouquet.

Getting the right balance between your outfit and the flowers means you shouldn't finalise your bouquet until after you have chosen your wedding dress. A large bouquet, for example, could overpower a simple or slinky dress, while a small, delicate posy will look unbalanced if you are wearing a full-skirted ballgown. Take a picture or at least a sketch of your dress along to show your florist.

Keeping the bouquet looking fresh can be a worry, especially in hot summer weather. Try to handle it as little as possible once it arrives, leaving it nestled in tissue paper and out of the sun. Contrary to popular belief, you shouldn't put it in the fridge since flowers don't like any extremes of temperature. Just as you leave for the ceremony, pinch out any bruised petals and gently fluff out the edges, which may have become flattened in transit. Always hold the bouquet slightly away from your body to prevent crushing the flowers or marking your dress.

During the reception, the bride's bouquet is usually placed at the centre of the top table or on the cake table.

Bridesmaids' flowers and the buttonholes

Your bridesmaids' flowers should echo the style and colour of your bouquet. The most popular option is to give each maid an identical posy. Alternatively, you could get each maid to carry their favourite flowers but all in the same colour.

Younger flower girls often enjoy carrying a small basket filled with flowers or petals to scatter down the aisle. If you don't want them to have to carry anything, ask your florist to design a floral bracelet or hair decoration. For tiny maids, a teddy wearing a fresh corsage is a sweet alternative and doubles as a thank-you gift.

Buttonholes always looks good on a dark suit and help to visually unite the whole wedding party. Popular flowers for buttonholes include roses, orchids, carnations and the smaller varieties of lily.

Your groom will probably want to have something slightly different from his best man and ushers, ideally a flower that's being used in your bouquet. Many couples leave a tray of buttonholes at the door of the ceremony for guests to help themselves. It's also a nice idea to give the fathers of the bride and groom a special buttonhole, and both mothers a corsage, though you will have to make sure they complement the outfits they will be wearing.

Styles of bridal bouquet

Hand-tied: Blooms wired together or casually hand-tied. They work best at a contemporary wedding with a simple dress.

Pomander: A tight ball of flowers, usually without foliage, suspended on a ribbon that the bride can hang from her wrist.

Posy: Small, simple and usually hand-tied with ribbon. Lily of the valley makes the perfect minimalist posy.

Round: The classic bouquet, usually consisting of larger flowers such as roses and peonies that are loosely arranged and then tied with ribbon.

Shower: A waterfall-like spill of flowers wired to cascade from a handle. This is the most traditional and formal of the bouquet shapes and suits full-skirted dresses.

Flowers for every season

Whatever the time of year there are so many beautiful varieties of flowers and a wealth of colours to choose from.

Spring

Amaryllis: A large, open flower perfect for larger bouquets and centrepieces.

Anemone: Available in about 120 different varieties. The brighter colours are great for trendy posies.

Daffodil: A bright yellow flower that is always popular for spring weddings.

Freesia: Small, highly scented flowers in bright colours. Ideal for headdresses and posies.

Gerbera: Large and dramatic daisy-like flowers that come in orange, red, pink and yellow.

Lily of the valley: Tiny, bell-shaped white flowers with a sweet fragrance. A classic wedding flower and ideal for small posies. Expensive, though.

Orchid: Exotic and pricey but available in a variety of pretty colours

Ranunculus: A buttercup-shaped flower popular for spring weddings. Available in a variety of colours.

Stephanotis: A traditional and popular small white wedding flower with a wonderful sweet scent.

Sweet pea: A classic wedding favourite with a sweet, lingering fragrance.

Summer

Anthurium: Famous for its glossy, waxy-looking flowers. Popular for beach and tropical themes.

Carnation: The traditional choice for a buttonhole and available in lots of colours. Also works well en masse in pomanders for bridesmaids.

Chrysanthemum: A versatile flower ranging from daisy-like flowers to large pom-pom shapes.

Gypsophila: Tiny white or pink flowers that form a cloud-like display. Best used in quantity.

Lily: There are about a hundred varieties in a huge range of colours.

Magnolia: Large, subtly scented flowers in a wide range of shapes and colours. Popular for reception decoration.

Peony: Large, fragrant flowers with petals in a bowl shape. A popular bouquet flower in pink or white.

Rose: The most popular of all the wedding flowers and used for bouquets and decorations. Available in a huge variety of sizes, varieties and colours.

Sunflower: A refreshing choice for summer. They can be pricey but are so big you won't need many.

Your Flowers

Autumn

Agapanthus: Large, bell-shaped flowers in a striking shade of violet. They add a splash of colour to bouquets and centrepieces.

Aster: A small, daisy-like flower in a wide variety of colours, usually with a bright yellow centre. Pretty in bouquets.

Clematis: Perfect for trailing bouquets. Available in a good selection of sizes and colours.

Daisy: An all-year-round favourite that always looks bright and cheerful. An ideal flower on which to theme your whole wedding.

Hosta: Not strictly a flower but a variety of popular foliage with heart-shaped leaves ranging in colour from soft to brilliant green.

Hydrangea: Large, full flowers in a variety of pretty pastel colours. Good for centrepieces and pedestal arrangements.

Passion flower: Large, exotic flowers that can be used to add splashes of bright colour.

Pinks: Not surprisingly, available in a variety of shades of pink – from very pale to almost red. Pretty round flowers that are ideal for bouquets.

Winter

Camellia: Beautiful open-faced flowers ranging from a single row of petals to overlapping multi-rows. Popular for buttonholes because of their richly coloured foliage.

Euphorbia: An evergreen shrub with yellowish flowers. Useful as an all-year-round addition to venue arrangements and more elaborate bouquets.

Iris: An unusual fan-shaped flower with three large petals. Usually blue, lilac, purple or white and popular for centrepieces.

Nerine: Sprays of hot or pale pink trumpet-shaped flowers. Fairly exotic, so good for unusual centrepieces.

Pansy: Small, flat-faced flowers in a variety of colours and intensities. Can be kept in the pot and double up as a table decoration and a pretty favour.

Snowdrop: A delicate white flower and one of the classic bridal blooms. Ideal in hand-tied posies and for smaller table decorations.

Tulip: A cheerful favourite available in a wide range of colours. The varieties with frilled edges are very popular for contemporary bouquets.

The meaning of flowers

Flowers have a language all of their own and you can
send a secret message of love to your groom.

Apple blossom	Perfection
Arum lily	Ardour
Azalea	True to the end
Bluebell	Lasting love
Camellia	Perfect loveliness
Carnation – red	Admiration
Carnation – white	Sweet and lovely
Daffodil	Joy
Daisy	Innocence
Forget-me-not	True love
Freesia	Sweetness
Gardenia	Purity and joy
Gerbera	Cheerfulness
Honeysuckle	Bonds of love
Iris	Hope and wisdom
Jasmine	Sensuality
Lemon blossom	Fidelity
Lily of the valley	Happiness
Mimosa	Sensitivity
Orchid	Beauty
Rose – pink	Happiness
Rose – red	I love you
Rose – white	Purity
Snowdrop	Hope
Stephanotis	Marital happiness
Sunflower	Adoration
Sweet pea	Lasting pleasure
Tulip – red	Love
Tulip – yellow	Sunshine of my life
Violet	Faithfulness

Your Flowers

Kate Smallwood &
Chris Bamford

Welcome Hotel
Stratford-upon-Avon

Chapter *11*

The Beautiful Bride

Every bride is a beautiful bride, but who doesn't need a little help in achieving perfection? This chapter is all about looking – and feeling – great from top to toe, as well as offering some invaluable tips on what to do if stress is in danger of affecting your day.

Start your journey to bridal perfection about three months before the big day. This will give you enough time to achieve some good results but not so much time that you lose interest and all your hard work goes out the window before the big day actually arrives.

Skin care

If you don't already have a good skin care regime in place, now is the time to start. It may be worth investing in a professional facial, particularly if you have problem skin, where you'll have an expert on hand to answer any questions you may have about what products and treatments will suit you the most. They'll also be able to advise you on what to use on your body as well as your face.

Get into the habit of cleansing, toning and moisturising your skin every day and having a facial every other week for a deep-down clean. This doesn't have to be a professional treatment; there are lots of products you can use at home that give very good results.

Use an exfoliating product in the shower to buff your body and smooth out dry skin areas such as heels, elbows and knees, then slather on lots of rich moisturising lotion for super soft and touchable skin.

Hair care

Hair can cause more stress to a bride than anything else, or more specifically how to wear your hair on your wedding day. Get some professional advice about three months before the wedding and ask your hairdresser for suggestions for what will suit you. Take along a picture of your dress to this consultation and chat through your headdress options and whether or not you'll be wearing a veil.

Your stylist will be able to try various looks for you to see what you feel comfortable with. It's a good idea to take a snap (a phone camera is ideal) of the style options, trying to get every angle so you can have a think at home about which look you like the best.

Your wedding is not the day to try out a radical new hair style of any kind. You don't have to grow your hair and if you don't usually wear your hair up, chances are you will feel very self conscious if you walk down the aisle with an elaborate up-do. And if you are usually a brunette, it's not a good time to try out those highlights you've been thinking about for the past year!

Real Bride's Hot Tip
❝I booked a make-up artist for my wedding. She did my maids make-up as well and was brilliant at calming us all down when we got the jitters.❞
Vanessa Aldridge, Edinburgh

What you should be aiming for is a perfected version of your usual style. A good cut and great condition will give you far more confidence than wondering whether your guests and, more importantly, your groom will like your new hairstyle.

A deep conditioning treatment once a week for a couple of months will quickly show good results and encourage a healthy shine. It's also a good idea to make an appointment for a trim in the week before the wedding. You may want to book your stylist for the wedding morning as well; it will give you one less thing to worry about on the day and there's nothing like a professional blow-dry to make your hair look great.

Make-up

Even if you hardly ever wear make-up in your everyday life, you'll need to wear some on your wedding day. If you don't, you run the risk of looking washed out in your photographs and that's not a good look for any bride!

Sign up for a make-up lesson or think about booking a make-up artist for your wedding morning if you don't have much confidence in your own ability. Most services include at least one pre-wedding trial where you can discuss different looks. Alternatively, brave the make-up counters in your local department stores. Most of the big brands such as Estée Lauder and Chanel have a bridal service and are nowhere near as scary as you might think! For a small fee you'll get lots of advice, a make-up session and usually many free samples to try out at home.

Essential wedding make-up

The make-up basics will go a long way towards looking good and even a make-up virgin shouldn't have too much trouble getting them right.

Concealer A good idea if you have the odd blemish. It should be applied before foundation.

All-in-one foundation and powder This comes in a compact format and you put it on with a sponge. It gives even coverage without adding colour and stops your face from looking shiny.

Blusher You shouldn't need much blusher – you'll probably have an in-built glow already. Why do you think they say 'the blushing bride?' For a light blush, sweep a little soft rose or peach powder across the top of your cheekbones using a large blusher brush.

Eyeshadow A little brown or soft grey eyeshadow lightly smudged across each lid will give your eyes depth and help them to look bigger.

Mascara Use eyelash curlers before mascara for a real eye-widening effect and – for obvious reasons – use a waterproof mascara. Brown is often more flattering than black for pale complexions.

Lipstick Choose a shade of lipstick in a soft pink shade with just a hint of glossy shine. Apply one coat, blot firmly on a tissue and then put on another coat for the longest-lasting effect.

The golden glow

Most wedding dresses reveal quite a lot of flesh and you'll want that skin to look good. Other than using lashings of rich moisturiser for a super-soft feel, the best way to boost the skin tone on your upper arms, chest and back is to invest in a light tan. Avoid the sun bed, which is not a skin-friendly idea at any time of the year. You need to fake it.

There are lots of DIY fake tanning products but your wedding day is not the time to chance streaks and a dodgy finish, so a professional tanning treatment is definitely recommended. This can either be applied with a spray gun or by hand and should give a believable result that lasts for anything up to a week, certainly long enough to see you through the wedding and into the first few days of your honeymoon.

Shape and tone

It goes without saying that you will want to look great in your wedding dress. But you also have to be realistic about what is achievable in the run-up to your wedding. Shedding a few pounds, flattening a wobbly stomach and toning upper arms can be done in about three months: dropping two dress sizes can't!

Real Bride's Hot Tip
66 *I joined Weightwatchers and lost 8lbs before my wedding. I knew I couldn't do it by myself and the support from other members made all the difference.*99
Sarah Watkins, Liverpool

Whether or not you want to lose weight for the wedding, starting a healthy eating regime is a good idea. Cut out as much sugar and processed food as you can, replacing them with lean meat or fish, fresh vegetables and salad. Cutting calories by 500 a day and taking a long walk a couple of times of week will result in a weight loss of two pounds a week and it will hardly feel like dieting at all. Also try to reduce your alcohol intake in the weeks before the wedding and get as much sleep as you can. Not only will a better diet pay dividends with your skin and hair but it will also give you more energy to face all those wedding planning tasks.

The stress factor

Weddings are stressful for everyone closely involved but are most stressful for the bride. Don't be surprised if you find yourself feeling tired, irritable and downright grumpy as the big day approaches – that's perfectly normal. You may even find yourself suffering from what is jokingly referred to as 'the bridezilla syndrome'– a state of mind that can overtake any girl who is planning a wedding, turning her into a bit of a monster!

If stress is starting to take its toll, recognise that you probably need some help with the wedding preparations. You are not superwoman and you can't juggle planning the biggest and most expensive party of your life, working full time and having a life without some assistance. Your fiancé may need to pull his weight a bit more; it's his wedding too and since he is likely to be the one bearing the brunt of your moods he should be more than happy to help out. Delegate some of the less important but essential tasks to your mother or a trusted and organised girlfriend. Get a second opinion from someone you trust if making so many decisions is keeping you awake at night.

And join the *You & Your Wedding* chat room at www.youandyourwedding.co.uk. Thousands of girls are going through exactly the same highs and lows as you are and who better to talk to than other brides?

Looking gorgeous in your wedding photos

Expert tips on how the supermodels look good in every picture.

- Never stand square to camera but stand slightly side-on; it will make you look slimmer.
- If it's hot, take a minute to dab on a little powder before your main photo session so you don't look 'sweaty' in all the shots.
- Your smile will quickly look false if you have to keep it up for too long. Every third picture, relax your face and give your mouth a little wiggle before saying 'cheese' again.
- Slightly tip your chin down as you smile; chin up will make your face look fatter.
- Ask to be photographed out of direct sunlight so you don't have to squint. Strong sunlight directly on to your face will also cast dark shadows under your eyes.
- Hold your bouquet in a relaxed position at thigh level. If you hold it too tightly under your bust, you'll look as though you are trying to hide a pregnancy.

*Becky Croucher
& Neil Jeffries*

*Kakslauttanen Igloo
Village, Finland*

Chapter *12*

Your Hen Night

The days of dancing round your handbag are long gone – the modern hen night is a much more stylish affair! But it is still your big chance to celebrate your upcoming nuptials, to let your hair down and forget about wedding plans for a few fun-filled hours.

Over the last ten years the traditional hen and stag nights have changed and these days you are much more likely to be planning a weekend celebration rather than just one night of partying.

Your chief bridesmaid usually shoulders the main task of arranging something that you will enjoy so, if you have a firm idea of what you would and wouldn't like to do, make sure you let her know in plenty of time. Just bear in mind that not everybody is earning the same amount and that your wedding is already costing the average guest a pretty penny in outfits, accommodation, taxis and a gift. An expensive hen event might be beyond their means!

Who to invite?
The guest list should include the bridesmaids, the bride's closest friends and relatives and usually the groom's closest female relatives as well. And only people who are invited to the wedding should be invited to the hen night. Whether to invite both mothers is really up to you, your relationship and what you are planning to do. If the hen event isn't the sort of thing your mothers will enjoy you can always plan a nice lunch with just the three of you so they don't feel left out of the girly goings-on.

It's a good idea for you and your chief bridesmaid to sit down and work out the guest list together so nobody gets inadvertently left out. Invitations can be verbal, emailed or written but make sure somebody takes charge of the RSVPs and is responsible for taking hotel deposits if necessary and ensuring the date, times and directions are all made clear.

When and where?

The hen night is usually planned for about a month before the wedding, depending on when most people indicate they are free to come along. Definitely don't plan to hold it during the wedding week; there will be far too many other things to think about to enjoy yourself.

Try to arrange the date for the hen night at least two months in advance so that everyone can save the date – co-ordinating diaries can be nightmare! It's much easier to pick the date early so you'll be the first in all their diaries.

When it comes to what to do, there are lots of interesting choices that will prove much more memorable than going to a club and drinking too much booze (although this is fine if it's what you want to do!). Think about the mix of people you will be inviting and what they will enjoy; it is much better to match the event to the people rather than the other way round. Your idea of a wild night out may shock some of your friends and you don't want a divided group with someone creating an atmosphere.

It is probably not a good idea to ask too many people for their suggestions for what to do; accept from the outset that you will never please everyone and it is what you want that matters most. Get together a small hen party 'committee' of three or four people and, once you have decided on the ideal format, it has to be a case of like-it-or-lump-it for the majority of your guests. They know it's what you want that is most important.

Real Bride's Hot Tip
We went into a recording studio for my hen night celebrations and made a pop video. We then played it at the wedding. It was the best fun and made a fab memento.
Denise Morrison, Cardiff

Some hot favourites for a modern hen night include:

- a pampering spa day/weekend
- visiting a comedy club
- a European shopping day/weekend
- a pole-dancing lesson
- a chocoholics cookery class
- going to a pop concert
- riding rollercoasters at a theme park
- driving a fast car (or even a tank) around a track
- disco-hopping in a limo
- a slumber party in a fancy hotel

The bride is generally not expected to have to pay anything towards her hen night, unless you have decided upon something very extravagant involving nights away. Usually the chief bridesmaid will ask the other guests to add 10 per cent on to any deposits or restaurant bills to cover your share and hopefully everyone will bring enough cash on the night so you don't even have to buy a round of drinks.

Hen night organiser's checklist

In consultation with the bride-to-be, make a list of intended guests.

Come up with a venue/event idea and a proposed date when most people seem available.

Plan an itinerary and book everything in advance so you are sure to get in. Pay any up-front deposits and ensure you know who has/hasn't paid.

Send out invitations mentioning the date, timings and also the expected cost.

To liven up the evening, ask guests to bring along old photos, props etc. – anything that will make a good story about the hen in her younger days.

Pre-book everything for the evening, making sure that any venues are happy to accommodate a large single-sex group (many are not).

Plan everything down to the last detail and make sure everyone has your mobile number; it is easy to get separated if you are moving from one place to another.

Arrange transport home (for you and the bride if for no one else!).

Hen night guests are expected to bring a small gift for their hen, which usually revolves around sex! Lingerie, fluffy handcuffs, tame sex toys... you get the picture. Hen nights have always involved a little bit of hen humiliation – and probably always will. But hopefully your friends are sensitive enough to know how far they can push it before it stops being fun.

A joint party

There is no reason why you can't celebrate your hen and stag nights together. Lots of couples do because they share many of the same friends and have the same taste in entertainment. Alternatively, you could start off separately, perhaps by having a meal, and then arrange to meet up in the local cocktail bar to compare notes.

Rules of the game

A lot of brides-to-be get very stressed about what they imagine their groom will be getting up to on his stag night and vice versa – girls on the razz can be equally badly behaved – so it's worth both of you reading through these simple rules before you head out to party.

- Talk to the best man and chief bridesmaid beforehand and let them know just where to draw the line. Be specific: if a stripper is a definite no-no, say so.
- Involve each other in your plans; keeping things secret will make it seem as though there's something untoward going on.

- Be sensitive to each other's feelings; if you know a strip club will send your other half crazy, don't go there. It really isn't worth the aggravation.
- On the night refuse to take part in anything that makes you uncomfortable or means you have to keep your behaviour a secret from your other half.
- Reassure your intended after the event that the only dodgy thing to come out of the evening was your hangover.

The bridal shower

One trend from America that is catching on in Britain is the bridal shower, where friends get together to 'shower' you with gifts and good wishes. It is much like an engagement party but just for girls. A shower is a great alternative if you don't want to have a traditional hen night or partying just isn't your thing.

The shower usually takes place in someone's home during the afternoon or evening and is generally a much more civilised affair than the hen night. Tea, cakes and nibbles are served, with perhaps a glass or two of champagne. Many brides have more than one shower, with their friends and their workmates holding separate events on different dates. Traditional shower gifts include linens, crystal, small china objects, wine and coffee-table books.

Hen night scattergories

There is nothing like a game to fill a quiet moment and get a group of guests who may not know one another that well laughing.

Make up game cards using eight or so wedding-related topics, such as flower, venue, first dance song and honeymoon destination. Put all the letters of the alphabet into a hat and draw out one letter each round. Everyone gets one minute to fill in each category with wedding-related words beginning with that letter. For the letter C for example, guests could write carnation, Cliveden, Can you feel the love tonight? and Cancun. Players get 1 point for every category correctly completed (it has to have a wedding theme) and 3 points for an answer so original that nobody else round the table thought of it. Once you've worked through the alphabet, tot up the scores and the winner gets a bottle of bubbly.

Lindi Mabena & Robert Pitts

South Africa

Chapter *13*

Your Gift List

Every one of your guests will want to mark your big day by giving you a present, so compiling a wedding list is something you should be considering. Although some brides worry about it, a gift list really is the only way to be sure of getting what you actually want!

The wedding gift list presents many couples with a bit of a dilemma. On the one hand you are probably thinking: 'What a great idea! Here's our chance to fill our home with lots of lovely new things': on the other hand actually telling your guests what you want them to buy all seems a bit… well, tacky.

There's nothing to say you have to have a gift list but do remember that most of your guests will want to buy you something. People enjoy giving gifts and will want to contribute to your home in celebration of your marriage. Without a list of specific items to guide them as they shop, your guests are faced with the unenviable task of trying to work out what you like and what is missing from your home. This is when you could possibly end up with a lot of things you don't like or need – a waste of time, energy and, above all, money.

Try to think of your gift list not so much as dictating what people should buy but as a guide to what you would like. There needs to be enough variety of items and price options that everyone will feel there's something on it they can reasonably choose for you. The average guest or couple will probably spend around £30–70 so you need plenty of items within this range. You also need to include a few cheaper ideas for children and guests who have travelled a long way, so have already spent lots of money just to be there on the day. You can also include a few more expensive items that several people may buy together. Work colleagues, for example, will usually buy a joint rather than individual gifts.

How does a gift list work?

A wedding list is just that – a list of items you would like to receive if people are feeling generous enough to buy them for you. It can be arranged through a department store, a specialist gift list company, online, or you can do it yourself.

The list is usually sorted three to four months before the wedding, sooner if you like, though details of the what, when and how need to be finalised by the time you send out your invitations. You should compile your list with your fiancé; shopping may not be his idea of fun but the gifts you choose are for you both, after all.

Before you start looking for specifics, try to make out a rough list of what you actually need. Gift list basics are linens, china, cutlery, towels, small electrical appliances, tools, picture frames and ornaments. This is your chance to replace older household items and treat yourselves to the latest designer gadgets.

Real Bride's Hot Tip
66*Make sure you include a wide range of prices on your list. We had things for £10 for my little nieces to buy right up to a £400 washing machine.*99
Amanda Morris, London

If you already have all the basics you need, there is nothing to say you can't broaden the present spectrum a bit and include sporting items, gym equipment and things for the garden. But do try to include items that your guests, and particularly the more traditional ones, will think are suitable for a wedding.

It is worth checking out the possible gift list options before picking one. The service offered by different department stores will differ and the brands they stock may not be the same. If you have your heart set on an item or a range by the latest hot designer, you'll need to make sure you are registered where it is stocked. This is where the web will come in very handy. Log on to the various shops and read through the gift registry section. It is also a good time to check that their service suits your requirements.

Your Gift List

- How is the list managed? The online services give the most flexibility for you and your guests.
- Can your guests order items online, over the phone and in person? Can they use credit cards?
- When do the gifts get sent out? Some ship all in one go after the wedding, others sent individual gifts as soon as they are purchased.
- Will items ordered months before the wedding actually be in stock after the big day when it's time for delivery, or will there be a long wait?
- Do they charge for delivery? Do they offer a gift-wrapping service?
- What is the returns policy if you don't like something or change your mind?
- Is there a deadline for when all gifts must be delivered after the wedding?
- How long will your list remain open?

Your gift list options

You have several choices when it comes to managing your list and which you choose will depend on the type of gifts you want to receive.

The department store

The easiest and most obvious place to put your gift list is with one of the major department stores. They are all managed much the same, though the ones with an online facility will make life easier for your guests because they can see what they are buying without going into the shop and usually order online and pay by credit card. You will be able to check your list online too, tracking what has been bought and whether you need to add more items, if you are proving popular!

Most stores have an in-store adviser who will show you what to do. You either get a clipboard and paper to walk around the shop jotting down the make, price and stock number of anything that you like or you use a hand-held scanner to zap the item barcode. All your chosen goodies are then put on to one master list with your names and wedding date.

The master list is held at the store and is updated as guests buy their gifts. Your gift list adviser will then send you regular updates as well so you can see who has bought each gift.

The store will probably give you a pack of branded gift registration cards once your list is sorted that state 'Amanda and Mike have their gift list at .... store', with contact details and a reference number. You can either pop one of these in with your invitations or wait until someone asks for your list details and then hand one over.

The specialist gift list company

This type of shop is dedicated just to wedding lists and you get a very personal service, perhaps goodies such as a glass of wine when you compile your list as well as online back-up. They usually offer a wider selection than a department store and can source more unusual items and expensive designer brands.

The management of the list is much the same as for a department store and you will get regular updates of how the list is progressing. Most specialist companies have a website so guests can see what they are buying, and they usually deliver all gifts in one delivery, on an agreed date, once the list is closed.

Do it yourself

There's nothing to say you can't manage your gift list yourself, particularly if you have a computer. Doing it yourself will give you maximum flexibility, enabling you to choose a wide range of items from a wide range of shops. This is a task that could also be taken on by a willing mother or friend; the master list should be held by one organised person who is available to send out a copy to anyone who asks for one, answer questions and keep up-to-date records as gifts arrive.

The main problem with a DIY list is knowing when items have been bought since, unless guests tell you they've bought something, you may find out only when it is delivered. The chance of duplicate gifts is high but as most shops have a refund or exchange policy this may not be an issue for you.

For something completely different

If you really don't need a lot of household basics then you may like to think about a list where guests pledge money towards something in particular. This can include your honeymoon – several of the major tour operators now offer 'honey money', where guests can put cash into a fund for you to spend on spa treatments, boat trips or even towards the cost of the trip itself. Or how about creating a whole new garden for your home? Garden centre gift lists allow guests to pledge money towards gardening equipment, trees and plants and sometimes a comprehensive design service as well.

If you'd rather your marriage celebration helped those less fortunate than you, a charity gift list is a lovely idea. Several of the major charities, such as Oxfam, operate a traditional wedding list where you choose a selection of items but instead of gifts for you they are useful things for developing countries. How good will it make you and your guests feel to think you have bought a fresh water supply for a village or school books for several children?

A question of cash

At one time it was considered the height of bad manners to even think about asking for cash rather than a wedding present. These days, with more and more couples already living together and no longer needing to buy all the household basics, it is not an outright no-no, but you do need to ask in the right way to avoid offending anyone.

Don't ask for cash with your wedding invitations but suggest that family and close friends spread the word that you would rather not have specific gifts at the moment. They could say if you are saving up for a new conservatory, for instance, or thinking about undertaking a major home improvement project in a few months' time when the cash would be very useful.

At all times it's important to stress that you don't expect any form of gift; your guests' presence at the wedding is enough but, should they want to get you something, money would be your preferred option.

If older guests don't feel comfortable about handing over a cheque – and many will feel this way – offer the option of gift or store vouchers, which seem less like money, and they will feel happier knowing their money will be spent on something you need for the future.

Present problems

Even if you have a wedding list you are bound to get given a few things you don't want and you will need to handle the situation with care.

You hate the present Having a gift list doesn't guarantee that one of your friends won't go 'off list' to give you something of their own choosing – and unfortunately we don't all share the same taste. If the giver is a close relative or friend who is likely to be a regular visitor, accept that you are going to have to keep their gift, albeit hidden in a cupboard and brought out for display every time they come round! On the other hand, if the giver is unlikely to be in your home very often and you know where the item was bought, ask to exchange it. Providing it's still boxed, there shouldn't be a problem.

The gift is broken If something you receive from your gift list supplier arrives broken, call the shop and tell them as soon as it arrives and ask for a replacement. If the gift was given on the wedding day, subtly try to find out if the giver used a credit card, in which case the card insurance should cover the damage and it can be replaced.

> ### Real Bride's Hot Tip
> *❝Make a list of who has given you each present. Don't trust your memory; you'll forget when it's time to write those thank you notes! ❞*
> **Sue Miller, Wittering, Sussex**

Duplicate gifts It's good to have several sets of sheets or towels but perhaps not necessary to have two or three toasters. Department stores will happily let you exchange goods and your guests will never know.

Saying thank you

You will want to say a personal and heartfelt thank you to everyone who has come to your wedding and generously given you a gift. A written thank you is expected even if you said thanks in person at the wedding.

Writing out 100-plus thank you cards is time consuming and it's a job that both you and your groom should tackle together. The easiest way is for you to thank your friends and family and for him to do the same for his. Split joint friends between you.

Send out thank yous as soon as you can after the gift has been received. If presents arrived before the wedding it's fine to send a thank you straight away. If you want to leave the thank you notes until after the wedding, they should be mailed within a month to six weeks; any longer and you run the risk of being considered rude.

Thank you cards need to be hand written – emails or photocopied sheets are not considered polite. You can buy packs of thank you cards from any high street stationer or you could ask your wedding stationer to make some cards in the same design as your invitations. Another nice touch is to make some simple folded cards showing your favourite snapshot from the wedding day.

Nobody expects you to write a masterpiece; you are simply thanking them for coming to help celebrate your day and for giving you such a kind and generous gift. You should personalise each card by mentioning the item received and perhaps saying how you may use it in the future. For example: 'Thank you so much for the fabulous toaster. I will think of you every morning when Michael serves me breakfast in bed!' If someone has given you money, try to give an idea of how the money may be spent, even if you have yet to decide.

Your Gift List

Jacqueline Wilson
& Paul Hanks

Ravello, Italy

Chapter *14*

Your Honeymoon

Wherever in the world you decide to go and whether you want a laid-back or an action-packed honeymoon, this is the first chance you'll have as a couple to relax, unwind and simply enjoy being married. So get ready to plan and enjoy the holiday of a lifetime!

Strictly speaking, your honeymoon begins with your wedding night – the first night you spend together as man and wife after the wedding. Chances are your honeymoon suite will either be at the reception venue or at a nearby hotel and you'll want to splash out on a really nice room to mark the occasion.

Make sure you have seen the room in person before you book, checking details such as the bed (a four-poster is traditional) and the bathroom (does the bath or shower have room for two?). Arrange for a bottle of chilled champagne and perhaps a late-night snack to be waiting on arrival; you will have had a long day and you probably won't have eaten much. For an extra romantic touch, ask the hotel to scatter petals across the bed and, if permitted, set out a few candles.

Once you have slipped away from your guests and the door is firmly closed on the marital bedroom, try not to feel under too much pressure to 'do it'. You may feel exhausted and one or both of you may have had too much to drink. Not having sex on the wedding night is more common that you might think and doesn't mean you love each other any less. Of course, you may feel like putting on a romantic CD and making passionate love; after making all those public vows this is your chance to be intimate. Just think. When you wake up there will be no pressure to do anything at all other than ordering breakfast in bed then diving back under the covers to enjoy another round of glorious married sex.

The honeymoon starts here

Planning your honeymoon is enormous fun. When else do you get to pick out some of the most romantic destinations in the world, then splurge on a trip and have everyone's blessing to pack up and go?

Give yourself plenty of time to arrange this all-important holiday – booking about six months in advance is usual. It sounds obvious but do check that both your passports are valid for the duration of the trip and six months beyond. If a new passport is necessary, apply for this well in advance. The Passport Office gets very busy during traditional holiday times and you need to allow for any delays.

Real Bride's Hot Tip

❝ *We didn't have sex for the week before the wedding so by the time the wedding night came along, we couldn't keep our hands off one another!* **❞**

**Kathleen Joseph,
Billericay, Essex**

If you intend to change your surname and will want to travel in your newly married name then you need to get your passport changed before the trip. You can do this up to three months in advance of the wedding, though you won't be able to travel using the new passport until after you are married. Check out the Passport Office website for more details (www.passport.gov.uk/passport_amending_marriage.asp).

It's important that your travel documentation and your passport are in the same name – it doesn't matter if you don't get round to changing your passport and travel using your maiden name; the two documents just need to match for the purpose of travel.

Decision time

Take a good hard look at your wedding budget and see what is realistically available to spend on your honeymoon. The UK average honeymoon costs about £3,000 but you can spend less – or a lot more. Enjoy an indulgent evening with a pile of brochures and surf the internet to compare prices. If there's a particular hotel that

appeals in a brochure, check out the prices on the hotel's website; you can often get good deals by booking this way, then all you have to do is buy a (hopefully) cheap flight.

Prioritise what matters to the two of you. For some a buzzy resort with lots to do is a must: for others seclusion and quiet is what appeals. Of course, you may not want the same thing from a holiday, in which case a two-centre trip may be the answer, with action to start and relaxation to finish (see page 195).

It's a long-standing tradition that the groom pays for the honeymoon, though these days it is more likely that both of you will be paying for the trip out of your wedding budget. It is also traditional for the groom to surprise his bride and choose the destination on his own. Fine if you trust his judgement, but it is probably safer to drop some heavy hints about what constitutes your dream trip. Spending a fortnight at a place that isn't quite what you had in mind won't be the best start to married life!

Getting the most from your honeymoon budget

- Shop around and ask at least three different tour operators for their best price. You'll be amazed at what you can save on the exact same trip.
- Get web-savvy while you search. You'll find more choice, and booking online often saves you at least 10 per cent.
- Include a Saturday night in your package to get the best air fares.
- Try to travel at off-peak times. This is not an option during the summer months but do ask, for example, about flying on a Monday or Tuesday rather than at the more popular weekend.
- Flight upgrades aren't usually forthcoming but you will stand a much better chance if you are smartly dressed.
- For a small fee you can use the business class lounges at some airports, even if you are flying economy. A little luxury will get you off to a great start!
- Think about travelling to Europe by boat or on the Eurostar and then hiring a car once you are in France.
- Up the luxury factor by staying fewer nights at a particular resort but in a better quality hotel.
- If you enjoy sports, check out all-inclusive packages where lots of activities are included in the one price, as well as most food and drinks.
- Avoid hotel restaurants – they tend to be pricey. Food is usually better locally.
- Tell everyone you are on your honeymoon; you never know what freebies may come your way!

> ### _Real Bride's Hot Tip_
> 66 _My groom organised a surprise honeymoon. It was a sweet gesture and I really had no clue where we were going until the airport. Luckily I love Barbados!_ 99
> **Monica Dooner, Camberley, Surrey**

Honeymoon health check

Find out what inoculations you need at www.netdoctor.co.uk or pick up a Department of Health E111 leaflet from your GP or local health centre.

To discover if a destination is safe, check the Foreign Office website at www.fco.gov.uk
Make sure you take out travel insurance before you go.

Questions to ask

Not everyone is an experienced traveller so before booking it's as well as to ask the experts about anything you feel could potentially spoil your trip. If you are using a tour operator or travel agent, take advantage of its expertise: if you are arranging the trip independently, check tourist board websites and accommodation details direct with the hotel.

❏ Is the area safe? Are there places we should avoid, particularly at night?

❏ Can we drink the water and eat all local food safely?

❏ Do we need inoculations or other health precautions?

❏ Are flights direct (stopovers can be exhausting)?

❏ What is the local currency?

❏ What is the local voltage (for your hairdryer, toothbrush, shaver etc.)?

❏ Would you recommend a hire car to get around?

❏ Can we request a special in-flight meal? Can we pre-book our seats?

❏ Are hotel transfers included in the price?

❏ Is there a special honeymoon package at the hotel?

❏ Can we request a special room such as the honeymoon suite or a sea view?

A world of romance

Once you've set your budget, the fun part is choosing where to go. The most important point is where in the world to travel to find romance – after all this is your honeymoon! Here are the top ten favourites guaranteed to get you in a romantic mood.

Amalfi Coast, Italy

This wonderful stretch of Italy's coastline is considered by many to be Europe's most romantic destination. Stretching from Sorrento to Salerno just south of Naples, it is dotted with picture-postcard villages stacked like wedding cake tiers into the hillside. Best of all is the drive along the snaking coast road with its stunning views of the Mediterranean.

Who to contact: Italian Connection (www.italianconnection.co.uk); the Italian Tourist Board (www.italiantouristboard.co.uk).

The Caribbean

The Caribbean islands offer masses of choice for island style as well as where to stay, with something for everyone from big resorts to intimate boutique hotels. The beaches and the weather are the two big attractions of the islands and this is a popular destination for anyone planning a wedding abroad. The paperwork is easy and the locations just about unlimited. Choose Antigua for beaches, Jamaica for nightlife, St Lucia for scenery, Barbados for old-world charm, St Barts for glamour and Anguilla for laid-back relaxation.

Who to contact: Caribtours (www.caribtours.co.uk); the Caribbean Tourist Board (www.caribbean.co.uk).

Fiji

The 300 lush islands in the South Pacific make it a wonderfully tranquil and adventurous place to hide away on your honeymoon. Yes, it is the other side of the world but the long trip is worth it for the unspoilt beauty of the place and the seclusion of the hotels. Its deserted beaches, clear blue seas and luxurious resorts make it the favourite holiday spot for many A-list celebrities. And don't worry; even though it is tropical country there are no poisonous snakes and no malaria to worry about.

Who to contact: Tailor Made Travel (www.tailor-made.co.uk); South Pacific Information (www.southpacific.org).

Koh Phi Phi, Thailand

The exotic appeal of Koh Phi Phi continues to draw couples eastwards. There are lots of other trendy destinations in the area but it's still Koh Phi Phi, with its combination of incredible beaches (*The Beach* was filmed here), laid-back nightlife and romantic resorts that attracts newlyweds. It is routinely voted as one of the prettiest islands in the world and is only 45 minutes from the airport at Phuket. A sure honeymoon bet.

Who to contact: Thailand Tourist Board (www.tourismthailand.org).

The Maldives

The coral-ringed stopping-stones across the Indian Ocean are a mecca for lovebirds seeking the honeymoon idyll of palm fringed, deserted white sand beaches. Choose your resort carefully if you're looking for activities; many of the resorts revolve around seclusion and offer little else than get-away-from-it-all relaxation. Pricey but undoubtably memorable.

Who to contact: ITC Classics (www.itcclassics.co.uk); the Maldives Tourist Board (www.visitmaldives.com).

Maui, Hawaii

Maui is incredibly beautiful and well worth the long trip to get there. The air is filled with the fragrance of tropical flowers, the beaches are golden and uncrowded and the water is warm and clear. The laid-back locals are another major attraction for visitors, as are the vibrant restaurants and the dramatic Haleakala Crater, an extinct volcano that is one of the coolest places on earth to watch the sunrise.

Who to contact: Hawaiian Holidays (www.hawaiian-holidays.co.uk); Hawaii Tourism (www.gohawaii.com).

New York, USA

New York has it all for anyone not interested in the beach. You can stroll through Central Park, shop for trinkets in Tiffanys, climb to the top of the Empire State Building, catch the ferry to Staten Island or take in a Broadway show and then dine in one the fashionable restaurants on Fifth Avenue. Throw in movie-set locations such as SoHo and some of the best hotels in the world and you have a dream destination.

Who to contact: Virgin Holidays (www.virginholidays.com); New York Tourism (www.nycvisit.com).

Your Honeymoon

Paris

Paris is so romantic it's almost a cliché. Thousands of couples cross the Channel every year to soak up this beautiful city's atmosphere. There is nothing quite like strolling along the Seine and kissing at the top of the Montmartre steps or at the top of the Eiffel Tower. Once you have seen the sights you can enjoy gourmet food in some of the world's best restaurants. The shopping is amazing too.

Who to contact: The French Tourist Office (www.uk.franceguide.com).

Scotland

There's no need to go far to find a heavenly honeymoon. Scotland has romance by the bucketful and attracts couples from far and wide to its scenic shores. If you love the notion of bracing walks by a stunning loch, deserted beaches, rolling Highland heather and ancient castles, this is the right place for you. Round off the day snuggling up in front of a roaring peat fire in your castle bedroom with a shot of whisky – and the fact that the weather is atrocious won't matter a jot!

Who to contact: The Scottish Tourist Board (www.visitscotland.com).

Venice, Italy

You won't have to try hard to find something romantic to do in Venice – the entire city is honeymoon heaven. Canals arched with pretty bridges replace roads, beautiful boats are used instead of cars and the haunting songs of gondoliers echo through the piazzas. The city has every size of hotel, nearly all of them wonderfully old, steeped in history and overwhelmingly romantic.

Who to contact: Magic of Italy (www.magicofitaly.co.uk); the Italian Tourist Board (www.italiantouristboard.co.uk).

The world's best beaches

- Pink Sands, Bahamas
- Maundays Bay, Anguilla
- Datai Beach, Langkawi, Malaysia
- Matira Beach, Bora Bora
- Le Morne Peninsula, Mauritius
- Wilson Island, Great Barrier Reef
- Maroma Beach, Mexico
- Woolacombe, Cornwall
- Denis Island, Seychelles
- Jumby Bay Beach, Antigua

Two-centre honeymoons

You like lazing on the beach but your man wants action and adventure: you want big-city buzz and he wants relaxation and quiet. Well, they say opposites attract and choosing your honeymoon destination could be the first test of compromise in your marriage.

Two-centre holidays are already popular and make the perfect honeymoon, usually combining two very different places so you feel you are getting two holidays for the price of one. Accept that one or both of you will have to give on certain aspects of the trip and there should be somewhere in the world that keeps you both happy.

Here are just a few suggestions for two destinations, not too far apart, that offer the best of both worlds.

Action	Relaxation
Big game African Safari	Flopping on a Mauritian beach
Skiing on Lake Tahoe, USA	Chilling in Las Vegas
Shopping in Miami	Driving through the Florida Keys
The sights of Sydney	The beaches and diving in Queensland
Clubbing in London	Log fires in the Cotswolds
A walking tour of Paris	A secluded Normandy château
Shopping and football in Madrid	The beaches of Marbella

Even if the two of you love lots of activities, it isn't a good idea to try and pack in too much on your honeymoon or to move hotels more than a couple of times. Weddings are stressful and you will be tired. Once the adrenalin has stopped pumping you may be surprised at just how exhausted you feel. If you are planning an action-packed start to your trip, try to build in a few days of doing nothing much at all towards the end – you don't want to return from your honeymoon feeling you need another holiday!

A happy honeymoon

You are bound to have expectations about your honeymoon – sun, sea and lots of sex – but don't expect it to be hearts and flowers every minute of the trip. That is just not real life and you don't want to suffer from the honeymoon blues.

⁶⁶Your honeymoon is so much more than just a holiday and needs to be filled with memorable moments.⁹⁹

It probably won't be your first time travelling together so you'll have a pretty good idea of whether your other half is a good traveller or not. Make allowances for the fact that you will both be tired and, having just experienced the biggest event of your lives, you may hit a low spot once you reach the calm of the honeymoon suite. The first couple of days of the trip are a good time to chat about all the wedding details, the highs and lows, which bit you both enjoyed the most and what didn't go quite according to plan. Once this is done, try not to talk about the wedding again. You have lived and breathed your big day for long enough and there is no going back, so try to put it all behind you – at least until you get home and see the wedding photographs!

Indulge each other with little surprises; take advantage of all the honeymoon extras that will probably come your way, such as a candlelit dinner, a romantic cruise, or spa treatments for two; simply revel in your newly married status. But don't feel you have to spend every waking moment together. If either of you wants to go for a run, a swim or a walk on the beach alone, enjoy it. Being married doesn't mean living in each other's pockets and you can still be independent, even if you are on your honeymoon.

Honeymoon checklist

- a valid 10-year passport
- travel insurance
- currency, including small notes for tips and taxis on arrival
- credit cards
- a voltage converter
- a list of important addresses and telephone numbers
- first-aid kit including insect repellent, arnica cream, analgesics (paracetamol, aspirin etc.), plasters and any medication you need while you are away
- mobile phones, camera

- vaccinations
- birth control
- a capsule wardrobe to make you feel special
- romantic CDs and sexy underwear
- luggage labels with both your home and hotel details
- sun protection, sun hats and shades
- pampering beauty products
- advance reservations for any spa treatments in case the hotel is super-busy

Amanda Clarke
& Ian Hallam

Blenheim Palace,
Oxfordshire

Chapter *15*

From This Day Forward

This is the chapter to read when your honeymoon is over, the whirlwind that was the build-up to the wedding and the day itself is past and you are probably more than ready to settle down into your new life as man and wife. But will it be happy ever after?

Being married is bound to involve a period of adjustment, even if you'd been living together before. It is a time when you have to make all sorts of decisions about money, domestic arrangements, even decorating styles and, instead of making these choices alone, you'll now have to consult your other half.

Post-wedding blues

Go on, admit it; even though the wedding preparations were manic and stressful you enjoyed being the centre of attention, didn't you? It was fun to have everyone talking about your wedding, anticipating your dress, wondering about the food and generally getting excited about every aspect of your big day. The wedding day itself may have passed in a blur but it was probably a wonderful blur, filled with moments of great joy and an overwhelming feeling of love and contentment. The honeymoon was blissfully romantic and everyone kept congratulating you on your newly married status. But the wedding is over, the excitement is over and it is back to reality. And reality can be a little bit humdrum so it's hardly surprising if you experience a few low moments in the weeks after the honeymoon.

In fact, it even has a name – the post-wedding blues! It's usually the bride who suffers the most from the blues because you were the one doing most of the wedding work; but your man could well be feeling the same. Instead of snapping his head off at the slightest thing when you are feeling down, explain how you are feeling and recognise that this mood will disappear within a month or so.

Have a couple of strategies in place for the first few weeks of married life to keep yourselves active, and arrange a few treats to look forward to – this will stop you constantly looking backwards.

- Arrange your first married dinner party for a few close friends.
- Book a romantic night or weekend away.
- Plan a night in to watch the wedding video with a bottle of champagne.
- Set yourselves a project, such as decorating the study or putting in decking.

    You don't have to start it straight away but the planning process is always fun.

Just the two of us

Compromise and humour are key to any successful relationship; so is making time for leisure and for your friends. Just because you are married your social life doesn't have to revolve around one another all the time. Spending the occasional evening or afternoon apart enjoying sport, a yoga class or shopping with your mates is even more important now than when you were single.

You love one another to bits but you still need some alone time. It may be that you need to set aside an hour or two a week to read a book or indulge in a spa bath and he needs to spend a couple of hours watching football or listening to music. Respect each other's space and don't feel hurt or rejected if he doesn't feel like being with you every minute of the day.

> ### Real Bride's Hot Tip
> 66 *At first I didn't get why he wanted a boys' night out but I've realised he's not out chasing other girls, just catching up with his mates.* 99
> *Denise Morrison, Cardiff*

It's also important to remember that the marital home belongs to you both so, if either one fancies inviting mates over for the evening, check that the timing is right for your other half. There are few things more annoying than coming home from a bad day at work, anticipating a quiet night in, to be faced with a horde of faces all looking to crack open the wine. Check each other's weekly diary on a Sunday evening so you can plan time together and time apart.

We are family

Parents, as well as friends can be a point of friction for some newlyweds. If you are from a super-close family, having your mother and sister popping round or calling every evening may seem normal to you; it may not to your new husband. It may be better to agree a time to meet for coffee at 'theirs' rather than at your home and offer to chat on the phone in your lunch hour at work.

Where you go on Christmas Day is another potentially tricky situation, particularly the first year after you are married. You either have to work out a visit to both sets of parents or, if distance makes this is impossible, it's a good idea to plan a trip abroad – which avoids the problem altogether!

Who does the domestics?

The domestic side of your marriage needs to be sorted once the honeymoon period is over. If you are both working you need to split the chores as equally as possible so one of you doesn't end up feeling resentful that they are shouldering most of the household tasks. Divide things up according to who can tackle it best: you may be more adept with the washing and ironing, while he enjoys mowing the lawn and is happy to do the washing up. Problems usually occur when one of you is much tidier and is constantly clearing up after the other. Try to set a few ground rules over what is acceptable, probably meeting in the middle on most things. Don't expect either you or your partner to change completely – that's not going to happen!

If something about your man is driving you crazy don't let it fester; talk about it. It is amazing how quickly things like leaving the top off the toothpaste and dropping wet towels on the bathroom floor become an issue. The sooner niggles are addressed, calmly and without shouting, the quicker they will be sorted. Chances are he may not even realise that it has been stressing you out at all.

The post-wedding to-do list

Much of your married life will probably feel just as it did when you were single but there are a few things to get sorted in the first few weeks of nuptial bliss.

Will you change your name?

For many women changing their name from the one they have used all their life seems a strange thing to do – and there's no reason why you have to take your husband's name if you don't want to. In fact, he can take your name if he prefers or you can join the two names together to create a new, hyphenated name. One popular compromise is for the newlywed woman to use her maiden name for work, where she's well known by that name, but to use her married name for anything socially and at joint events. If you have children you'll need to decide which name they will take but it is usual for the children to take on the father's surname to avoid too much confusion.

Your husband's parents may take a dim view if you decide not to take 'their name', but explain early on that it is important for your work that you use your maiden name and it really is nothing personal.

If you have changed your name, you need to let the appropriate people know. Write to your bank, building society, mortgage lender, credit card companies, the human resources department at work, your tax office, doctor's surgery and anywhere else that regularly contacts you and needs to address you correctly. If you haven't already done so, arrange to change your name on your passport; the relevant form is available from the Post Office.

What about your finances?

What's mine is mine and what's yours is yours is one way of looking at what you will bring to the marriage, or you could decide to pool everything and agree that you share it 50/50. It all depends on how much each of you has accumulated in the past. If it involves a lot of money or property it may be worth taking legal advice to protect your investments.

If you are both working you may or may not want to pool all your money into one account. Joint accounts for household expenses, mortgage payments and paying general bills is the simplest option, with you both paying an agreed amount into the fund by standing order every month. But each of you will probably want to maintain a separate account for personal expenses such as clothes, hobbies and small purchases that you don't want to have to keep explaining to your other half.

> ### Real Bride's Hot Tip
> ❝We use our joint account for all the bills but have our own money for everything else and it's no questions asked as to how we spend it!❞
> *Mary Norden, Norwich*

If you don't already have things such as medical insurance, household insurance, pensions, regular savings and life cover, getting married is a good time to think about how these could benefit your life in the future. In the event of something happening to either of you, you need to be sure that the mortgage will get paid and that any children you have will be adequately provided for.

Any Will you made before your marriage will automatically have been revoked, so you should think about making a new one to take account of your newly married status as soon as possible after you are married.

❝*A happy marriage takes work but the rewards are well worth the effort.***❞**

Happily ever after

You will probably find this hard to believe but at some time in the future, married life might start to feel all a bit boring. The love notes will have stopped, you won't be spending Sunday mornings indulging in marathon sex sessions and you probably won't feel the urge to talk to your man on the phone every half an hour. Job deadlines, domestic chores and even a baby will become a priority and you will need to stop and remember why you got married in the first place.

Routine is fine – it is how most people manage their lives – just as long as it isn't boring. Make time for each other and try to surprise one another occasionally by initiating something that is definitely not part of your usual routine.

- Book a romantic night or weekend away and stay in the room for the whole time.
- Invite your man on a date. The rules are that you have to dress up and act as though it is the first time you have ever met.
- Have sex somewhere other than the marital bed; indulge in some slow, sensual foreplay; take a bath together; massage each other or make love by romantic candlelight.
- Eat together as often as possible. Even a simple meal with a glass of wine can be made to feel special.
- No matter how busy your diaries, make time to talk to one another. Turn off the TV and pay attention to each other's work worries and be sensitive to each other's moods.
- Try never to go to sleep in a bad mood with each other.

And that's just about it. Hopefully this book has helped answer at least some of your wedding-related questions, eased just a little of that pre-wedding stress and has set you on the right road to not only a wonderful wedding but also a wonderful married life. Good luck!

From This Day Forward

Your Wedding Directory

www.youandyourwedding.co.uk is the perfect wedding website, whether you want to work out your budget, arrange your seating plan, find great suppliers or just chat to other brides in the chat room. It is invaluable!

Accessories

Angela Hale Jewellery
020 7495 1920
www.angela-hale.co.uk

Butler & Wilson
020 7409 0872
www.butlerandwilson.co.uk

Coleman Douglas Pearls
020 7373 3369
www.astleyclarke.com

Dominic Walmsley Jewellery
020 7250 0125
www.dominicwalmsley.co.uk

Emma Hope Shoes
020 7259 9566
www.emmahope.co.uk

Halo Headdresses
01694 771470
www.shropshirebrides.co.uk

Jimmy Choo Shoes
020 7235 0242
www.jimmychoo.com

Joyce Jackson Bridal Veils
01745 343689
www.joycejacksonveils.com

Meadows Bridal Shoes
01603 219174
www.meadowsbridalshoes.co.uk

Polly Edwards Tiaras
01903 882127
www.pollyedwards.com

Rainbow Club Shoes
01392 207030
www.rainbowclub.co.uk

Cake makers

Betty's of Harrogate
01904 659142
www.bettysbypost.com

British Sugarcraft Guild
020 8859 6953
www.bsguk.org

Celebration Cakes
01189 424581
www.celebcakes.com

Choccywoccydoodah
01273 329462
www.choccywoccydoodah.com

Elizabeth Lyle
01892 740354
www.elizabthlylecakes.com

Konditor & Cook
020 7261 0456
www.konditorandcook.com

Linda Fripp
01722 718518
www.lindafrippcakes.co.uk

The Little Venice Cake Company
020 7486 5252
www.lvcc.co.uk

Maison Blanc
020 7224 0228
www.maisonblanc.co.uk

Pat-a-Cake-Pat-a-Cake
020 7485 0006

Peggy Porschen Cakes
020 7738 1339
www.peggyporschen.com

Purtia Hyam
01403 891518
www.chocolateweddingcakes.co.uk

Rachel Mount Cakes
020 8672 9333
www.rachelmount.com

Savoir Design
020 8788 0808
www.savoirdesign.com

Catering companies

Admirable Crichton
020 7326 3800
www.admirable-crichton.co.uk

Blistering Barbeques
020 7720 7678
www.blisteringgroup.co.uk

Bovingdons
020 8874 8032
www.bovingdons.co.uk

Create Food
01883 625905
www.createfood.co.uk

Delectable Feasts
020 7585 0512
www.delectablefeasts.co.uk

Jalapeno
020 7639 6500
www.jalapenolondon.co.uk

Mosimanns Party Service
020 7326 8344
www.mosimann.co.uk

Norman & Hatwell Caterers
01963 362856
www.normanandhatwell.com

Urban Kitchen
020 7286 1700
www.theurbankitchen.co.uk

Chair covers and linens

Dandy Events
01912 722006
www.dandyevents.co.uk

Elite Weddings
0845 602 8851
www.eliteweddings.co.uk

Host With Style
020 8893 4823
www.hostwithstyle.co.uk

Northfields
020 8988 7977
www.linenforhire.com

Snape Drape Hire
01568 616638
www.snapedrape.co.uk

Dress designers

Alan Hannah
www.alanhannah.co.uk

Amanda Wakeley Sposa
www.amandawakeley.com

Berketex Bride
www.berketexbride.com

Browns Bride
www.brownsfashion.com

Caroline Castigliano
www.carolinecastigliano.co.uk

David Fielden
020 7351 0067

Ian Stuart
www.ianstuart-bride.com

Morgan Davies
www.morgandavieslondon.co.uk

Pronovias
www.pronovias.com

Pronuptia
www.pronuptia.co.uk

Suzanne Neville
www.suzanneneville.com

Veromia
www.veromia.co.uk

Watters & Watters
www.watters.com

The Wedding Shop
020 7838 1188

Florists

Angel Flowers
020 7704 6312
www.angel-flowers.co.uk

British Florists Association
0870 240 3208
www.britishfloristsassocation.org

Flower and Plant Association
020 7738 8044
www.flowers.org.uk

Jane Packer
020 7486 1300
www.jane-packer.co.uk

Mary Jane Vaughan
020 7385 8400
www.fastflowers.co.uk

Mathew Dickinson
020 7503 0456
www.mathewdickinsonflowers.com

Paula Pryke
020 7837 7373
www.paula-pryke-flowers.com

Wild at Heart
020 7704 6312
www.wildatheart.com

Gift lists

Debenhams
www.debenhams.com

Harrods
www.harrods.com

John Lewis
www.johnlewis.com

Marks & Spencer
www.marksandspencer.com

The Wedding Shop
www.weddingshop.com

Wrapit
www.wrapit.co.uk

Hen nights

Big Weekends
0870 744 2251
www.bigweekends.com

Hen Heaven
0870 770 1996
www.henheaven.co.uk

Party Bus
0845 838 5400
www.partybus.co.uk

Wicked Weekends
0870 774 0153
www.wickedweekends.co.uk

Hire companies

Host With Style
020 8893 4823
www.hostwithstyle.co.uk

Jones Catering Equipment Hire
020 8320 0600
www.joneshire.co.uk

Rayners Hire
020 8870 6000
www.rayners.co.uk

Spaceworks
0800 854 486
www.spaceworks.co.uk

Top Table Hire
01327 260575
www.toptablehire.com

Honeymoons and weddings abroad

Abercrombie & Kent
0845 070 0610
www.abercrombiekent.co.uk

British Airways Holidays
0870 850 9850
www.britishairways.com

Caribtours
020 7751 0660
www.caribtours.co.uk

Elegant Resorts
01244 897222
www.elegantresorts.co.uk

ITC Classics
01244 355527
www.itcclassics.co.uk

Kuoni
01306 747007
www.kunoi.co.uk

Virgin Holidays
0870 990 8825
www.virginholidays.co.uk

Menswear (to hire and buy)

Burton Menswear
0870 606 9666
www.burtonmenswear.co.uk

Debenhams
020 7408 4444
www.debenhams.co.uk

Ede & Ravenscroft
www.edandravenscroft.co.uk

Favourbrook
020 7491 2337
www.favourbrook.com

Gieves & Hawkes
www.gievesandhawkes.com

Hire Society
0870 780 2003
www.hire-society.com

Marc Wallace
020 7731 4575
www.marcwallace.com

Moss Bros Hire
020 7447 7200
www.mossbroshire.co.uk

Ozwald Boateng
www.ozwaldboateng.co.uk

Pal Zileri
020 7493 9711
www.palzileri.com

Pronuptia
01273 323046
www.pronuptia.co.uk

Young Bride & Groom
www.youngbrideandgroom.co.uk

**Young's Hire at Suits You
and Suit Direct**
020 8327 3005
www.youngs-hire.co.uk

Photography

**British Institute of Professional
Photography**
www.bipp.com

Master Photographers Association
www.thempa.com

**Society of Wedding & Portrait
Photographers**
www.swpp.co.uk

Speeches

Fine Speeches
www.finespeeches.com

**MJ Consulting Speech Making
Courses**
01314 666051

Utter Wit
www.utterwit.co.uk

Wedding Speech Builder
www.weddingspeechbuilder.com

Write 4 Me
www.write4me.co.uk

Stag nights

Big Weekends
www.bigweekends.com

Blokes Only
www.blokesonly.com

Extreme Activities
www.extreme-activities.com

Great Experience Days
www.greatexperiencedays.co.uk

Last Night of Freedom
www.lastnightoffreedom.co.uk

The Stag Company
www.thestagecompany.com

Stag Weekends
www.stagweekends.co.uk

Stationery

Belly Button Designs
01614 489333
www.bellybuttondesigns.com

CCA Stationery
01772 663030
www.ccagroup.co.uk

Hitched
www.hitched-stationery.co.uk

Scrumptious Design
0870 240 6672
www.scrumptiousdesign.co.uk

Silver Nutmeg
01992 501464
www.silvernutmeg.com

Smythson of Bond Street
020 7629 8668
www.smythson.com

Susan O'Hanlon
01753 887659
www.stationery-wedding.com

Toastmasters

National Association of Toastmasters
0845 838 2814
www.natuk.com

Transport

American Dreams
www.americandreams.co.uk

Antique Auto Agency
www.antique-auto-agency.co.uk

Bespokes Car Hire
www.bespokes.co.uk

Blue Triangle Buses
www.bluetrianglebuses.com

Elite Helicopters
www.elitehelicopters.co.uk

Historic and Classic Car Hirers' Guild
www.hchg.co.uk

Karma Kabs
www.karmakabs.com

The Marriage Carriage Company
www.themarriagecarraigecompany.co.uk

Starlite Limos
www.starlitelimos.co.uk

Wedding planners

Alison Price
020 7840 7640
www.alisonprice.co.uk

Carole Sobell
020 8200 8111
www.carolesobell.com

Deborah Dwek
020 8446 9501
www.deborahdwekweddings.co.uk

Kathryn Lloyd
020 7828 5535
www.kathrynlloyd.co.uk

Siobhan Craven Robins
020 7481 4338
www.siobhancraven-robins.co.uk

Supreme Events
020 7499 3345
www.supremeevents.co.uk

Wedding Bible Events
01235 538126
www.weddingbible.co.uk

Wedding shows

The Designer Wedding Show
www.designerweddingshow.co.uk

The National Wedding Show
www.nationalweddingshow.co.uk

The UK Wedding Shows
www.theukweddingshows.co.uk

Your Wedding Budgeter

You will want to keep track of your budget every step of the way. First, put in the estimate column the amount you would ideally like to spend on each part of the wedding. Once you have actually paid for something put this amount in the 'actual' column and the difference in the third column. You can then see at a glance whether you are overspending.

Category	Estimate	Actual	Difference + or −

Ceremony

Licence fee			
Location fee			
Officiant's fee			
Bell ringers/organist			

Wedding outfits

Bride's dress			
Headdress			
Veil			
Accessories			
Shoes			
Lingerie			
Hair			
Make-up			
Groom's outfit			
Accessories			
Bridesmaids' dresses			
Accessories			

Rings

Bride's wedding ring			
Groom's wedding ring			

Reception

Location fee			
Rentals (linens, chair backs etc.)			
Food			
Waiting staff			
Wine			
Champagne			
Soft drinks			
Evening bar			
Cake			
Favours			

Flowers/decorations

Ceremony decoration			
Bride's bouquet			
Bridesmaids' bouquets			
Buttonholes			
Corsages			
Centrepieces			
Cake table flowers			
Reception venue flowers			
Flowers for the mothers			

Music

Ceremony musicians			
Reception musicians			
Evening band/DJ			

Photography/video

Photographer's fee			
Videographer's fee			
Prints/video			
Disposable cameras			

Stationery

Save-the-date cards			
Invitations and RSVP cards			
Stamps			
Order of service			
Seating plan			
Place cards			
Menus			
Thank you cards			

Transport

Bride's car			
Bridesmaids' and mother's car			
Groom's self-drive car			
Shuttle bus			
Parking fees			

Miscellaneous

Wedding organiser			
Wedding insurance			
Attendants' gifts			
Tips			
Other			
Other			
Other			

Allow 5–10 per cent of the total budget for unexpected expenses.

You can also use an online version of this budgeter once you are registered at www.youandyourwedding.co.uk

Your Wedding Checklist

Everything that needs doing and when you should (ideally) be doing it.

As soon as possible

- ❏ Tell relatives and close friends of your plans.
- ❏ Place an announcement of your engagement in the local newspaper.
- ❏ Arrange the first meeting with your minister, priest or rabbi to set the date.
- ❏ If it is a civil ceremony, book the register office/civil venue.
- ❏ Set the budget and ask parents if they would like to contribute.
- ❏ Choose your best man, chief and other bridesmaids and other attendants.
- ❏ Decide on the number of guests and draw up a guest list with both sets of parents.
- ❏ Visit possible venues.
- ❏ Post save-the-date cards, if required.
- ❏ Discuss menu options with caterers, hotels and restaurants and get estimates for the food and drink.
- ❏ Make all reception bookings.
- ❏ Start looking for your wedding dress and attendants' outfits.
- ❏ Begin a beauty regime.
- ❏ Book your photographer and videographer.
- ❏ Organise wedding insurance.

Three months before

- ❏ Arrange a second meeting with your minister, priest or rabbi to discuss the service and agree the dates for the publication of the banns. If the ceremony is in a church other than the Church of England, notice of the marriage must be given to the superintendent registrar.
- ❏ Choose the hymns, music and readings for the ceremony.
- ❏ Choose and order the wedding stationery.
- ❏ Book the musicians for the reception.
- ❏ Choose a florist and have an initial meeting to discuss all the flowers.
- ❏ Order the wedding cake.
- ❏ Arrange wedding dress fittings and shop for the bridesmaids' dresses and accessories.
- ❏ Discuss your hairstyle with your hairdresser.

- ❏ Book your first night hotel (if different from the venue).
- ❏ Book your honeymoon.
- ❏ Check passports and arrange any inoculations.
- ❏ Choose your wedding rings.
- ❏ Book wedding cars.
- ❏ Organise your gift list.

Two months before

- ❏ Finalise your order of service and order the printed version.
- ❏ Reconfirm all prior bookings in writing.
- ❏ Post invitations with gift list details.
- ❏ Send out thank-you notes as gifts arrive.
- ❏ Buy all your accessories.
- ❏ Check the groom and best man have organised their outfits.
- ❏ Choose presents for all your attendants.

One month before

- ❏ Book hairdresser and make-up appointments for the morning of the wedding.
- ❏ Make sure everyone involved in the wedding knows what is happening and the timings.
- ❏ Write to banks and other official bodies if you are changing your name.

Two weeks before

- ❏ Try on your full wedding outfit and practise walking in your shoes.
- ❏ Confirm the number of guests with your caterer and draw up a seating plan.
- ❏ Order travellers' cheques and any currency for the honeymoon.
- ❏ Enjoy your hen night – and get your groom to hold his stag night in plenty of time.

One week before

- ❏ Arrange a rehearsal at the ceremony venue, if required.
- ❏ Confirm all reception arrangements in writing.
- ❏ Confirm the photographer, florist, transport etc., with timings.
- ❏ Type up a list of any must-take shots you want and send it to the photographer.

- ❑ Type up a favourite music play list for any DJ or band, including your first dance song.
- ❑ Check that the groom, best man and your father are all preparing their speeches.
- ❑ Think about a bride's speech.

The day before

- ❑ Help to decorate the reception venue, if necessary.
- ❑ Arrange for the cake to be delivered to the reception.
- ❑ Pack for the honeymoon and have the cases sent to the reception venue.
- ❑ Have a manicure.
- ❑ Relax and have an early night.

On the big day

- ❑ Make sure you give yourself plenty of time to get ready.
- ❑ Have all bouquets and buttonholes delivered or send someone to collect them.
- ❑ The mother of the bride and any bridesmaids leave first, followed by you and your father (or whoever is giving you away). The groom and best man arrive separately, usually at least 15 minutes before the bride.
- ❑ It is the best man's job to ensure that everyone has transport between the ceremony and the reception.
- ❑ Speeches usually come after the food and before the coffee. The bride's father speaks first, then the groom and the bride if she wants to. The best man speaks last.
- ❑ Traditionally the bride and groom leave the reception before all the other guests (though these days many couples stay with their guests until the end of the evening).

There is an online version of this checklist at www.youandyourwedding. co.uk. It can be updated and also has a handy notes facility.

Photographic Credits

With grateful thanks to all the photographers and real couples who contributed pictures to this book

Photographic Credits

Contents: Page 5 Lovegrove Photography (www.lovegroveweddings.com)

Congratulations: Page 6 Lovegrove Photography (www.lovegroveweddings.com)

Chapter 1: Page 8 Page Teahan (01258 817961, www.pageteahan.com); Page 11 Adrian Briscoe/Country Living UK; Page 13 Studio 33/You & Your Wedding UK; Pages 14 & 23 Lovegrove Photography (www.lovegroveweddings.com); Page 15 Packshot Factory/You & Your Wedding UK; Page 21 Lulu Guinness (020 8483 3333, www.luluguinness.com); Page 25 Ryan Sullivan/You & Your Wedding UK; Page 26 Jake Curtis/She UK

Chapter 2: Page 28 Lovegrove Photography (www.lovegroveweddings.com); Page 33 David Clerihew/She UK; Page 34 Elizabeth Zeschin/Good Housekeeping UK; Page 35 PSC Photography/You & Your Wedding UK; Page 36 Jeremy Hudson/You & Your Wedding UK

Chapter 3: Page 38 Lovegrove Photography (www.lovegroveweddings.com); Page 43 Stoke Park, Buckinghamshire (01753 717171, www.stokeparkclub.com); Page 44 Lovegrove Photography (www.lovegroveweddings.com)

Chapter 4: Page 50 Freeman Photographics (020 8989 9954, www.freemanphotographics.co.uk); Pages 56 & 59 Lovegrove Photography (www.lovegroveweddings.com)

Chapter 5: Page 64 Lisa Devlin Photography (01273 231047, www.devlinphotos.co.uk); Page 67 Page Teahan (01258 817961, www.pageteahan.com); Page 70 Le Manoir Aux Quat' Saisons, Oxfordshire (01844 278881, www.manoir.com); Page 71 Ashworth Photography (01638 601571, www.ashworthphotography.co.uk); Page 74 Foto Theme/Cosmopolitan UK; Page 75 The Royal Pavilion, East Sussex (01273 292813, www.royalpavilion.org.uk); Page 77 Raffles Resort Canouan Island, Grenadines (0845 070 0614, www.abercrombiekent.co.uk)

Chapter 6: Page 78 Rachel Barnes Photography (01832 720154, www.rachelbarnes.co.uk); Page 80 Lizzie Orme/Best UK; Page 83 Peter Dürkes/You & Your Wedding UK; Page 85 Cosmopolitan UK;

Page 86 Lovegrove Photography (www.lovegroveweddings.com); Pages 87 & 88 PSC Photography/You & Your Wedding UK; Page 89 Leith's (020 7614 4444, www.leithsat.com); Page 90 Bottom left: Claire Richardson/Country Living UK, Centre: Memory Bus (01628 825050), Bottom right: The Wedding Carriage Company (07071 711811, www.theweddingcarriagecompany.co.uk); Page 92 Adrian Briscoe/Country Living UK

Chapter 7: Page 94 Adrian Neal (01763 289703); Page 97 Joey Toller/You & Your Wedding UK; Page 98 Sian Irvine/You & Your Wedding UK; Page 99 Benoit Audureau/Zest UK; Page 101 Michael Paul/Good Housekeeping UK; Pages 104 & 107 PSC Photography/You & Your Wedding UK; Page 105 Peggy Porschen Cakes (020 7738 1339, www.peggyporschen.com) Photographs/Georgia Glynn Smith; Page 108 Foto Theme/Company UK; Page 109 Oliver Gordon/Prima UK; Page 111 Tara Martin/She UK; Page 112 Rachel Barnes Photography (01832 720154, www.rachelbarnes.co.uk)

Chapter 8: Page 114 Theodore Wood (020 8390 5071, wwww.theodorewood.com); Page 117 The Designer Wedding Show (www.designerweddingshow.co.uk); Page 119 Studio 33/You & Your Wedding UK; Pages 122 & 125 Lovegrove Photography (www.lovegroveweddings.com); Pages 123, 124, 129, 131, 134 & 135 PSC Photography/You & Your Wedding UK; Page 127 Charnos at figleaves.com (www.figleaves.com); Page 132 Victorio & Lucchino (www.victorioylucchino.com)

Chapter 9: Page 136 Klarke Caplin (020 7231 8118, www.klarke.com); Page 145 Peter Dürkes/You & Your Wedding UK; Page 146 Pen Heaven (www.penheaven.co.uk); Page 147 Robert Holmes/You & Your Wedding UK

Chapter 10: Page 148 Lovegrove Photography (www.lovegroveweddings.com); Page 151 Sian Irvine/You & Your Wedding UK; Page 152 Paul Tansley/Prima UK; Page 155 Sian Irvine/You & Your Wedding UK; Page 157 Jon Whitaker/You & Your Wedding UK, Sian Irvine/You & Your Wedding UK, Peter Dürkes/You & Your Wedding UK; Page 161 PSC Photography/You & Your Wedding UK; Freenaturepictures.com

Chapter 11: Page 162 Stephen Swain (www.stephenswain.com); Page 165 Lovegrove Photography (www.lovegroveweddings.com) or The Designer Wedding Show (www.designerweddingshow.co.uk); Page 166 PSC Photography/You & Your Wedding UK; Dennis Pedersen/You & Your Wedding UK; The Designer Wedding Show (www.designerweddingshow.co.uk); Page 169 Theodore Wood (020 8390 5071, www.theodorewood.com)

Chapter 12: Page 170 Charlotte Beech (www.whereintheworldischarlie.com) and Nick Meek (www.nickmeek.com); Page 174 Tara Martin/She UK

Chapter 13: Page 176 Joe (www.joe.co.za); Page 179 Kitchenaid (08456 049049, www.johnlewis.com); Page 182 Heal's (020 7896 7590, www.heals.co.uk/giftlist), Jasper Conran at Debenhams (020 7408 4444, www.debenhams.com), Next (0870 142 4141, www.nextweddings.co.uk); Page 183 Pen Heaven (www.penheaven.co.uk)

Chapter 14: Page 184 Lovegrove Photography (www.lovegroveweddings.com); Page 187 Wilson Island, Australia (0870 166 2070, www.austravel.com); Page 189 Top left: Hotel du Vin, Henley-on-Thames, Oxfordshire (01491 848400, www.hotelduvin.com), Top right: One&Only Palmilla, Mexico (www.oneandonlyresorts.com), Bottom left: One&Only Le Tousserok, Mauritius (www.oneandonlyresorts.com), Bottom right: Kichwa Tembo, Kenya (www.ccafrica.com); Page 190 Parrot Cay, Turks & Caicos (www.parrrotcay.como.bz); Page 193 Top left: Hotel Santa Caterina, Italy (0870 909 7554, www.citalia.com), Top right: The Oberoi, Mauritius (www.oberoi-mauritius.com), Bottom left: Royal Malewane, South Africa (www.royalmalewane.com), Bottom right: One&Only at Rethi Rah, Maldives (www.oneandonlyresorts.com); Page 194 PSC Photography/You & Your Wedding; Page 196 Bora Bora Lagoon Resort (wwww.lhw.com/BoraBoraLagoon)

Chapter 15: Page 198 Stuart Bebb (01869 242294, www.stuartbebb.com); Page 202 Mike McClafferty/She UK; Page 204 Lucy Pope/Prima UK; Page 205 Studio 21/Zest UK

For Your Wedding Notes

For Your Wedding Notes

Index

Page numbers in **bold** indicate major references

Index